Rise and be Healed

Freedom from Alcoholism / Addiction

by
Craig L. Bradley

authorHOUSE™

1663 LIBERTY DRIVE, SUITE 200
BLOOMINGTON, INDIANA 47403
(800) 839-8640
WWW.AUTHORHOUSE.COM

First published by AuthorHouse 01/11/05

ISBN: 1-4208-1728-0(e)
ISBN: 1-4208-1727-2 (sc)
ISBN: 1-4208-1726-4 (dj)

Library of Congress Control Number: 2004099696

Printed in the United States of America
Bloomington, Indiana

This book is printed on acid-free paper.

PREFACE

Let me thank you for purchasing this book. The funds collected from the sales of this book will be used to expand our efforts toward helping others learn how to help themselves open the door to a new and more meaningful life.

Craig L. Bradley

DEDICATION PAGE

This book is dedicated to my loving parents, whose unselfish love and support, made it possible for this book to be written.

Table Of Contents

Chapter One

BECOMING ALCOHOL AND/OR DRUG FREE

My desire is to help others who, like myself, have suffered great misery as the result of extensive alcohol and drug use, to come to understand and *know* that they *do not* have to continue living the way they are living. What is presented herein is a personal presentation of my experience, strength, and hope.

The following are some of the methodologies we will examine throughout this publication:

1. We will help the suffering person learn how to accept responsibility for their own recovery.

2. We will assist the recovering individual in confronting their own behavior, which has repeatedly resulted in undesirable effects on themselves, family, friends, and co-workers.

3. We will assist in recognizing the need for family involvement in recovery.

4. The recovering person's perception of reality is totally different than the one who does not suffer from this malady. The recovering person's thinking will change progressively, as he/she remains drug/alcohol free and uses the tools of recovery that are discussed in this text. Our dysfunctional behavior did not manifest itself overnight and neither will our recovery. It takes time to learn what the tools of sober living are and to become proficient at using them.

For the most part, everyone beginning the journey toward this new life feels somewhat unique, in that they are sure no one knows how they feel; how terrible their behavior has been in the past, or how justified they might feel for doing what they are doing. In most cases, we feel that if we were to trust anyone with the secrets of the 'real us', no one would understand and/or certainly not like us very much.

None of us come into recovery qualified for sainthood, nor are any of us likely to win any mental health awards. The truth of the matter is that most of us have similar histories of inappropriate behavior, some of which has been destructive and/or illegal; failed relationships, inability to have intimate friendships; employment difficulties; generally unsound and unreliable decision-making. I could go on and on listing difficulties of survival that we, as alcoholics struggle with. There is one common bond that we all have, when arriving at that point of taking action, **RECOVERY** that is, that we all earned a Masters Degree in **PAIN**, both physically and emotionally.

This publication will not try to argue with you about what you feel or think. By all means, you are entitled to think and feel however you do. But, if you are tired of thinking and feeling the way you do, this publication will teach you how to give yourself an opportunity to change *all* of that.

JUST DON'T GIVE UP BEFORE THE MIRACLE HAPPENS!!

5. We will examine other community resources that will assist you in recovery.

6. The reader will begin to learn the basic language of recovery: Primary, Progressive, Chronic, Fatal, and Bankruptcy (Spiritually, Mentally, Physically, and Emotionally).

7. If you are feeling helpless and/or hopeless, at this point, it's okay. What is normal for where you are right now is feeling confused and swamped with difficulty. The **GOOD NEWS** is that everything discussed here is a **PROCESS** that takes some time. As you go through each step or process, you become prepared for the next one.

Keep in mind that the learning and changing is, indeed, a process---not an overnight occurrence. The process will allow your thinking to become clearer and more focused. Your feelings will mend and change. Essentially, what will happen is that your skin will be *tougher* and your heart will get *softer*. Really! Our recovery will allow us to get in touch with many feelings we didn't know we had, as well as sort out all of the feelings we presently have.

8. We will examine some symptoms that are easily understood by the newcomer to sobriety:

    a. **Isolation:** Chemically dependent people either look up or down on other people. Isolation is broken when we meet on common ground.

    b. **Denial System:**
       "I don't have a problem."
       "I can quit whenever I want to."
       "If everyone would just leave me alone, I'd be fine."
       "If your wife/husband/boss did this, this, and this, you'd stay buzzed, too!"

3

The dynamics of our disease **DEMANDS** denial!!!

At first, we must realize that our thinking is not very trustworthy. We suffer from a disease which breeds irrational thinking, based on bruised emotions. Being able to admit to ourselves that we **DO** have a problem is **MAJOR** progress for us. **ADMITTING** it and **ACCEPTING** it are two entirely different things.

We must be able to admit to ourselves and perhaps to someone else that we, indeed, have a problem. In most cases, lurking in the back of our mind, is that **DANGEROUS NOTION** that we may, *some day*, be able to drink or drug successfully. This idea must be **gotten rid of!!!**

This is what happened to me. I looked back over the 24 years of my drinking and drug use and saw, clearly, that I didn't get into trouble every time I drank or used drugs. However, every time I got into trouble or had serious problems, I had been drinking or drugging---or both. Over the years, the pain began to outweigh the gain.

When I got to **RECOVERY,** I had long since passed the point of using and drinking to *'party'*. I was using and drinking---*just to function!* I shook so badly that I had to roll a joint and keep it by my bed, at night, so that in the morning, I could hit the joint a couple of times--- *first thing*---to slow the shakes enough---so that I could go to the refrigerator and suck down a beer as fast as I could---*just to relieve the shakes.*

I had to put the beer on the kitchen counter. Sitting on a bar stool, I had to put one of my children's straws in the beer. I gripped the beer with both hands on the can, elbows on the counter, and sucked it down as fast as possible. That was my every morning routine the last two years of my madness.

I had, long since, lost the ability to be a husband to my wife. I had become a dictator. I had lost the ability to be a father to my children and became a tyrant. My children never knew what to expect. I was liable to come home in a happy, generous mood with flowers and gifts or just as likely to come home shot or cut up from an evening of what had become 'normal' ignorance.

I was fortunate that I had grown up with loving parents, in what was an average household. My parents saw to it that I grew up in the church with basic Christian values. As my disease progressed, I eventually turned my back on everything of spiritual value. At one time or another, I compromised every principle I had grown up believing in. Eventually, I became a prisoner in my own skin. Inside was a warm, caring person, but outside I was running wide open--full of fear and anger. I could write a very large book about the horror stories of my life, but chances are, you have *'been there'---done that'* or you are well on your way to *'getting there---doing that'*.

STOP NOW!!

THE ENDLESS CIRCLE OF MADNESS
ALCOHOLISM and ADDICTION

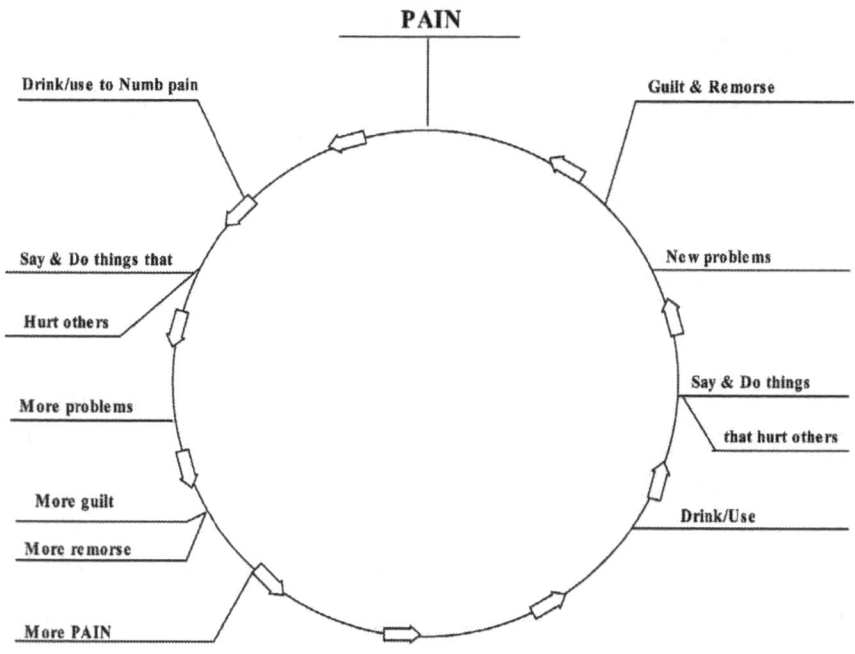

The Endless Circle of Madness

of Alcoholism & Addiction

For me, acceptance was looking back and realizing that my life had become an endless circle of madness.

I could quit whenever I wanted to.

My problem was staying quit!

I would stop drinking but use more drugs.   Then, I'd stop using drugs to end up drinking more. *From experience, I found that one leads to the other.* After countless failed attempts at trying to practice **controlled drinking** and **controlled drugging**, I realized that I was only fooling myself. I did not like myself or what I had become. The guilt and remorse was kicking my butt and the only way I knew how to deal with it was to numb-out so I wouldn't feel the pain. I had all kinds of good intentions about giving up the booze and the drugs in hopes of becoming a better parent and husband.

I did not know that my body chemistry had changed and it did not process alcohol and drugs like it used to. I had physically and mentally deteriorated to a point that no matter how much, *in my heart*, I wanted to stop, **the truth was** that I **COULD NOT—NOT USE** or **NOT DRINK**.

I did not know how to stop---and stay stopped!!

Thanks to God and the caring people of my immediate recovering community, I was **taught** how to stop and **STAY STOPPED**. Acceptance, for me, means that to pick up **a** bottle of beer or smoke **one** joint would just start that cycle of madness all over again.

Folks, I know what **HELL** is like—**BEEN THERE!!** For you who have also *been there*, no explanation is necessary. For those of you who have not been there, no explanation is possible.

I have **ACCEPTED** the fact that I have an allergy to alcohol and drugs. I said that to a friend once and he asked me what happened to someone who is allergic, if they use or drink anyway. I told him, "I break out in spots like Denver, Cincinnati, and Atlanta---followed by a rash of ignorance."

I finally stopped fighting the fact that I had a problem and began to *educate* myself about the problem, which led me to **SOLUTIONS** that I could understand. I'm not implying that they are at all easy to apply. With help, we learn how to understand and apply the solutions that have worked for nineteen million other people in the U.S.A. alone.

    c. **Delusion:** Delusion is defined as a system of thinking that supports denial. *"It isn't true, but it is logical."* Believing things to be so that are just *not* so. **Example:** After six or eight beers, I believed that I was as good looking as any movie star and/or as tough as any martial artist. **Problem:** After a few more beers, I would set out to prove it.

    d. **Value System: A Code of Conduct---Family, School, Church, Work, and Peer Relationships.** Simplified Explanation: If we stay within our value system, we feel **good** about ourselves. If we deviate from our value system, we feel **guilt and remorse.** If we make amends for the violation of our values, then we again feel better about ourselves.

No longer can we blame others or situations for our drinking and drugging problems. We begin to accept the fact that:

We are not bad people, trying to be better. We are people with a DIAGNOSABLE and TREATABLE DISEASE trying to get well.

Of course, some of our behavior might have been bad, but we learn to put that in the past. As we remain clean and sober, we learn how to replace old behavior with new and healthier behavior. It is a process of healing and repair that *DOES OCCUR, IF WE LET IT!!* We must become willing to follow the suggestions of those who have been where we are and have survived the lifestyle--those who moved forward to *SOBRIETY* and a *NEW LIFE!!!!*

THE PROCESS OF GETTING
FROM WHERE YOU ARE TO
WHERE YOU MUST BE

The Process of Getting from where you are to where you must be:	
Where you are now	Where you must be
Crisis	Feel the pressure
Assessment	Total Abstinence
Treatment/Recovery Plan	Develop confidence in the recovery process Become willing to follow suggestions
Treatment/Recovery Experience	Keep it Simple Stay busy
Psychological	Devloping more heightened Levels of Awareness
Emotional	Developing Acceptance
Spiritual	Personalization
AA-NA-ACOA-Alanon	Commitment to Recorvery

Chapter Two

ALCOHOLISM AND ADDICTION: THE DISEASE

(FOUR ABSOLUTES:PRIMARY, PROGRESSIVE, CHRONIC, and FATAL)

PRIMARY:

Most of us have other problems, physical and/or emotional, as well as our addictive disorder. **Primary** means that our first attention and efforts must be focused on becoming **TOTALLY** abstinent from using all mood-altering substances. Drinking and using drugs sets the stage for all of the other difficulties we have. **None** of our other difficulties can be effectively dealt with, *until* we get completely free of the drugs and alcohol. When this occurs, our minds and bodies begin to slowly return to some degree of normalcy.

Most of our lives had evolved around using drugs and/or drinking to the point that we had little to do with family and friends who did not *party* the way we did. We did not attend social functions unless we could drink or use our drug of choice. If we had to attend a function where drinking or drugging wouldn't be going on, we would drink or use before we got to the function. We would usually keep some with us or in our vehicle so we could take an occasional toot, while at the function. Eventually, everywhere we go and everything we do revolves around the availability of our drink and/or drugs. It becomes the *PRIMARY* topic that occupies our minds.

Whenever I had to take a trip out of town, I would gauge the trip, not in miles or hours of travel, but instead by how much beer I would need for the trip. Before I left work in the afternoons, I would ask myself if there was enough beer, in the refrigerator, to get me through the evening. I would usually stop by a store and get some anyway---*just to be sure I didn't run out*. If I began to run low during the evening, you could bet that I would send my wife to get more **BEFORE** I ran out. Maybe you can relate to this a *little---or---maybe* you have not gotten to this point---*YET!!!*

The most important message associated with **PRIMARY** is that when arriving at the point of recovery, we usually have acquired or developed other physical and emotional problems, other than alcoholism and addiction. None of those other problems can be effectively solved or dealt with successfully until the *"chemical"* problems are first dealt with. It is the addiction problem that sets the stage for the lifestyle that causes the other problems. So, changing the lifestyle is absolutely necessary for recovery to begin. This is one reason we say that recovery is a process, because we are not capable of changing our lifestyle overnight. We learn from others in recovery how to do this one step at a time. Most of those other problems straighten themselves out, when we stop drinking and using drugs. Your abstinence from all mood-altering chemicals **MUST** be your primary focus at first.

PROGRESSIVE:

Progressive simply means, that left untreated, our situation will only get *worse---never better.* One of the signs of early addiction is that it takes considerably more alcohol or dope to get us to the state we are accustomed to being in. We eventually lose the ability to achieve that special euphoric-type of high. We go straight from buzzed-to-trashed with no in between. We usually don't realize how messed up we are, until we have to speak or walk. Of course, if we are with people who are as messed up as we are, we have less of an idea of how blasted we really are.

Eventually, our body chemistry changes some more. Again, there is a noticeable difference in the relation to how much we use/drink and the degree of high we attain. It begins to take less of the substance to get messed up worse than usual.

That is why a wino can stay blasted all day on a two-dollar bottle of wine. His/her body chemistry has changed and deteriorated to the point that it no longer processes alcohol the way it used to. Therefore, it takes much less to get all screwed up.

When this change occurs, he/she is on very dangerous ground. When they discover that they are not getting as high, they will assume that the dope isn't as good a quality as they had been using. So what do they do normally? **They use TWICE as much**. This frequently results in an overdose. They are actually using a drug that is of normal or usual strength, thinking that it has been cut. When they instinctively use more than the usual amount, they **overdose**.

An overdose usually affects the lungs first. It acts as a massive sedative. Because the lungs are muscles, they become so relaxed that they literally stop working. Then the heart goes into overdrive trying to jump-start the lungs. The result is usually a severe heart attack or severe stroke---either of which, can and usually does, result in death for the victim of a hard drug overdose. For you hard drinkers, the same thing, can and does occur, when too much alcohol is ingested in too short a period of time.

You may be saying to yourself:

"I'm not that bad." or
"I'll stop before I get to that point."

I'm here to tell you, my friend, that by the time you get close to having this type of problem, you **WILL NOT** have the physical ability to determine when or how much you use or drink! If that were the case, 86% of the population would not have a problem with some type of substance abuse, which includes abusing prescriptive drugs.

I have a friend who is a successful businessman and a leader in his community. This friend did not believe he had a drug problem until we went through his desk and found thirteen (13) different prescriptions for Valium. Several of those prescriptions were open-ended and could be refilled whenever he chose. Staying mellowed out on Valium, all of the time, is just as much a problem as alcoholism or any other type of addiction.

The substance, itself, is not the problem. It has become our **SOLUTION!** There comes a time when it just doesn't work anymore and it begins to work **AGAINST US**---causing many types of problems.

OUR REAL PROBLEM IS OUR THINKING, which DEFINITELY needs to be changed.

In active addiction, we do not have the ability to be objective about ourselves; much less, change our thinking. We need help to begin this *process.* Without help, of some kind, our situation will only get worse. If you think this is an exaggeration, take a good look around you. Chances are that you know several people who have a problem with alcohol and/or drugs. Chances are you knew some of them before their using became a problem for them. Take a cold, hard look and **THINK!** If you think it can't or won't happen to **YOU**, you are sadly mistaken.

CHRONIC:

Once our body chemistry has deteriorated to the addictive state, we have usually developed a life-style that promotes continued use and a state of mind that demands continued use. **Chronic** means that once we have gotten into a recovery, we can reactivate the phenomena of craving, *at any time*, by using or drinking *just one time*. It is not uncommon to see someone who has been clean and sober for a number of years, relapse in a big way.

Example: If a person who has been clean and sober for five years decided that he could have *just one*, within a few short days, this person would be in the same physical and emotional state he would have been if he had never stopped at all.

When that monkey gets on your back, if we give in to it, Each time, it will take us further down the road than we have been.

Each time a relapse occurs, it becomes increasingly more difficult to get back on track. By far, the majority don't make it. Statistically, thirty-eight (38) people die from this disease for every one (1) who makes it to recovery. Those of us who make it to recovery should be *grateful* that we were not 1 of those 38 who did not make it.

Another frightening statistic is that out of every one hundred (100) people who attempt recovery, only three (3) will achieve long-term sobriety. I'm not trying to frighten you or discourage you---just the opposite! I'm trying to impress you with the **FACT** that if you are going to be successful at your attempt to recover, you are going to *HAVE TO USE ALL THE TOOLS OF RECOVERY*, not just the ones that apply to you. It was your thinking that got you in this mess. If you were baking a pie and decided to leave out some of the ingredients, common sense would tell you that it won't taste like it should. Likewise, our recovery and survival depends on our willingness to use *ALL* of the tools available to us. *Remember this:* God has provided a way out of our madness, as long as we remain grateful for our recovery and willing to follow some simple directions.

YOU *CAN* MAKE IT, BUT IT WON'T BE *YOUR* WAY AND "<u>YOURSELF</u>" WON'T DO IT!

This disease is cunning, powerful, and patient. It used to be referred to as *baffling*; however, between the wonderful progress modern medicine has made and the 67+ years of successful experience given to us by Alcoholics Anonymous, much has been learned about alcoholism and addiction. The more we learn about this killer and crippler, the better our chances of recovering.

I know that there is another drink sitting on that bar, waiting for me, but by God's grace and my using all the tools of recovery that I've been *taught*, I am able to push that drink into tomorrow. When tomorrow gets here, I do the same things:

PRAY, DON'T DRINK, GO TO A MEETING, and TRY TO HELP ANOTHER SUFFERING PERSON.

If I continue to do those things each day, I will be able to push that drink into tomorrow, *ONE DAY AT A TIME*.

I have not used any kind of mood-altering substance since the 14th of December 1987. I am thoroughly convinced that my recovery is the direct result of God's grace and my willingness to become teachable---then following the directions that were given to me by those who have gone before me. By observing others in my immediate recovering community, I know quite well how close I am to returning to a worse state of mind and body than I was in when I found recovery.

Today my life is full, busy, and joyful. It is not without the normal difficulties of life; however, in sobriety I have been given a greater quality of life than I could have ever imagined. All I have to do to lose it all is to pick up that *first* drink and I would be hell-bent on destruction.

Chronic also means forever and ever, Amen! It means that I will never again be able to drink or use drugs responsibly. I respect this fact and I **don't** live thinking in terms of *never* or *forever*. I just don't drink or drug *TODAY*. Those todays add up much quicker than you might think.

My true desire is to offer you *HOPE* for a successful recovery, but also to emphasize how insidious this disease really is. Chances are I don't have to explain to you the extent of damage this disease does to us and those we hold dear to us as well as those who have become victims of our less than wholesome behavior.

There are some who will read this material that have not progressed to the degree of insanity and unmanageability that some of us have reached. For those who are playing around with this *poison* in the name of *partying or just unwinding*, I am telling you that it *WILL* escalate into a *LIVING NIGHTMARE!* So, *STOP NOW!*

FATAL:

This disease absolutely guarantees that we will end up in jails, prisons, mental institutions, or *MORGUES*. It is hard to comfort our aging loved ones, if we are locked up or *dead*. God has a plan for you to rejoin the world of the living. Most of us who suffer from this disease die without ever giving themselves a fair chance at having a *NEW LIFE*. I'm nobody special folks---just a garden-variety drunk and junkie that, at some point, was told that I didn't have to continue living that way. I was told that I really did have a choice. If I could get clean and sober, so can *YOU!!!!*

YOU ARE NOT ALONE NOW!!!

Chapter Three

ORDER OF RECOVERY: Physical, Mental, Emotional, and Spiritual

PHYSICAL:

It is suggested that we begin our sobriety with a medically supervised period of detoxification. It is important that you realize unsupervised detoxification can be, and frequently is, dangerous. Most cities have detoxification facilities, as well as hospitals that will assist in this process. Detoxification usually takes three or four days, during which medication is usually administered to help the person's system adjust gradually.

After the initial period of detoxification, the person will likely feel tired, weak, and a little shaky. This is normal; uncomfortable, but normal for a while. Remember that *YOU* are responsible for your recovery. So, be prepared to start doing some things that will help your body adjust to functioning without the drugs or alcohol. As much as possible, begin to eat a more balanced diet and make yourself get plenty of rest. Also, make yourself exercise a little or participate in some form of physical activity. Don't over do it.

If in the beginning you have feelings of craving, this will usually pass quickly, if you eat some chocolate. If you are allergic to chocolate, then eat some other kind of candy. Don't try to figure it out right now, *JUST DO IT!!!*

Keep in mind that your body will go through a few different types of readjustments that can cause you some grief, if you don't know what to expect. What I'm trying to do here is to help you understand, *ahead of time,* what you can expect so that you will realize that some of what you experience is **normal** for early recovery.

One such experience is **sleep dysfunction**. There will probably be a short period of time when you have been active all day and are very tired; yet when you go to bed, your eyes won't want to remain shut and your mind will be racing a 100 miles per hour. You may wonder if you will ever get a full night's sleep again. Do *not* be alarmed! This will pass in a short time. On the flip side of this, you may be eating, exercising, and resting enough---but you begin to feel that you want to sleep all of the time. Both of these experiences are quite normal during early recovery. As your body chemistry begins to repair and stabilize, you will get back to a normal sleep pattern.

Many people interpret sleep dysfunction as a sign of depression and prematurely seek a physician's assistance in dealing with depression. This is usually done with mood- elevating drugs. The premature use of such drugs can, and frequently does, lead to relapse. It is natural, at first, to feel a little depressed. Let's face it, we have just given up our best friend, dope and alcohol. It was always there to take away our fears and make us feel better about ourselves.

Alcohol and drugs had become so much a part of everything we did. Now, all of a sudden, we are feeling feelings that we used to numb out. Now we are entering into a life having to learn how to socialize and function productively without the *"old friend"*. It is normal to grieve *"its"* absence and it is normal for you to feel some confusion about *"what to do next"*.

First, you must remember that what used to be an **old friend** is now a **new enemy**, which has begun destroying our lives and the lives of those close to us. Don't be afraid of the many types of feelings you will experience. They are a normal part of our body chemistry readjusting. However, if you are experiencing morbid depression after staying clean and sober for a year or so, then it would be a good idea to seek medical treatment for depression. Just don't be too quick to go that route in very early recovery.

MENTAL STABILIZATION:

Developing new levels of awareness...

As your body chemistry begins to repair itself, you will begin to experience different types of pleasurable excitement and enthusiasm about what you are discovering. You will come to realize, that after a few months of remaining clean and sober, that your ability to read and remember what you read will increase significantly. It is amazing how intensely we become tuned into our own basic instincts and senses. We begin to smell, taste, think and, in general, feel much better about ourselves. At first, there are conflicting thoughts about the unknown and a new life of sobriety---with the old thoughts of what is familiar. Some people hold on to the old thoughts, simply because we know what to expect. Part of early recovery involves learning how to *"LET GO"* of our old thinking and step forward into the **NEW**---with whatever degree of faith we can muster. That faith in the **RECOVERY PROCESS** comes as the result of prayer and observing others who are also in the same **PROCESS** and are experiencing some success.

Our mental attitude begins to change, because we realize that all of the fears and difficulties we face in our recovery program, are the same fears and difficulties that others in our community are dealing with. As we begin to grow and change, we will begin to experience some profound and wonderful discoveries about ourselves.

If you are a musician, artist, craftsman or whatever you do, you will begin to see, for yourself, that you will do everything better when you have been clean and sober for a little while. Your levels of proficiency, creativity, insight, and stamina will increase. You will also discover that you have interests and talents that you truly did not know you had. Your mind will continue to reveal, to you, special talents and abilities that the drugs and alcohol kept hidden from you. It is in your new recovering community that you will learn how to use those newly discovered talents and skills.

This period of self-discovery is very important in our new lives. We begin to realize that perhaps we are not as brilliant or talented as we perceived ourselves to be. Yet on the other hand, we discover that we weren't as burned out as we felt we were. We also discover that we are capable of learning more and moving on to higher levels of accomplishment. As new interests begin to develop, we begin to realize that whatever we had accomplished in our lives was a result of applying what we had learned someone at some point *TAUGHT US THE THINGS THAT WE KNOW.*

So, at this point, we look at where our old lifestyle has taken us and what our lives have amounted to. If we want our lives to *BE* different, then we must first *LEARN* how to *THINK* differently. There is no better or more effective way to accomplish this than by surrounding yourself with people who have already been where you are and have moved onto a more functional and spiritually mature manner of living and thinking. That is the basic purpose of 12-step support groups. There is a saying in recovery:

"We have to give it away to keep it.".

This means that the greatest insurance against relapse is prayer and working vigorously with a person new to recovery. As we work with a newcomer, it forces us to return to the **BASICS,** which got us sober and have kept us sober.

Newcomers frequently feel that they are bothering other people when they call or ask someone for help. **ABSOLUTELY NOT!!!** When a newcomer allows another person in recovery to help them with their recovery, **BOTH** people benefit. Realizing the need we have to let other people help us is a major step toward becoming **TEACHABLE.** We need to forget what we thought we knew about living life and allow those who have been sober awhile teach us how to live a sober life.

EMOTIONAL STABILIZATION:

This begins to occur, when we begin to accept our own humanity. We begin to accept the fact that, as human beings, we are perfectly imperfect. We all have character defects and shortcomings that guarantee that throughout life, we will periodically make judgment calls that are not as sound as we initially believed them to be. Sometimes, we simply make poor choices and have to learn to live with the consequences of those choices. The longer we remain clean and sober, the better our decision-making process becomes.

In active addiction and early recovery, our decisions are made based on what we *FEEL,* as opposed to a balance of what we *FEEL* and what we *THINK*. Emotionally, we are all pretty beaten up, when we get to recovery. Therefore, our emotional state is very fragile and super-sensitive. When faced with situations that are difficult or frightening, we have a tendency to look for a quick fix; that which is less demanding, less confrontational, less stressful, and which requires less time and effort. From life experience and general knowledge, we may very well know what the right thing to do is; however, in the newness of our sobriety, we simply are not emotionally strong enough to apply it and see it through. This is normal in early recovery, and it is important that you realize what is occurring in your own thinking process.

A trustable decision is made when we evaluate what we think and feel about something, and *then* make our decision based upon a balance of the two. Regardless of what you may think right now, it is important that you trust me when I say to you that *NO ONE* in active addiction and early recovery is capable of making decisions based on this balance that we are talking about. The reason for this assertion is because the neurochemistry of the brain is so screwed up. For a while, we are not capable of maintaining consistent emotional stability. We will discuss this further in another segment of this publication. For the moment, just understand that there are certain aspects of your recovery that require time to correct.

SPIRITUAL GROWTH:

True spiritual growth takes a clear mind and disciplines that we have to acquire or reacquire after having been sober for some time. It is usually the last and certainly the most important aspect of our new life. At first, we must stay sober to come to some understanding of our spiritual necessities. After maturing a little in sobriety, we grow to understand that we must stay focused on our spiritual growth, in order to remain sober. Whatever spiritual or religious beliefs we once had were compromised and distorted, as the result of our alcoholism and/or addiction. Many of us, eventually, return to the faith of our youth with greater understanding and a strong desire to become more Godly people. Those who had little or no religious or spiritual background, come to know the existence of a very real realm of spiritual matters. Before recovery, what we had was distorted opinions. The critical sarcasm was, perhaps based on judgmental attitudes, fueled by an incomplete picture and very damaged emotions. Our lives, as recovering people, depend on our willingness to eventually explore and grow in this area. With continued sobriety, we progressively become more willing to develop and redevelop in this area. If we fail to enlarge our spiritual life, relapse is eminent. Just as the other aspects of our recovery, we should seek guidance from those who have gone before us. Choose wisely those whom you ask to be your spiritual teachers, but *DO* make that choice! It is difficult, at any age and stage of our life, to admit to ourselves that we really need someone to teach us what we thought we already knew. With a little sobriety and a lot of willingness, we can become teachable once again.

WE HAVE BEEN DOING THE BEST WE COULD WITH WHAT WE HAD TO WORK WITH.

What have we been working with? We've been working with fragile, bruised, and super-sensitive emotions. The emotional state was caused by the lack of proper neuro-chemical brain functioning, which has resulted as the direct result of alcohol and/or drugs in our system.

Chapter Four

A GENERAL OVERVIEW OF THE PART PLAYED BY OUR NEURO-CHEMISTRY

There are certain chemicals in the brain called endorphins, which act as neurotransmitters. They carry electrical impulses designed to do a specific job in the brain. There is a chemical which, when produced, gives us a feeling which in large doses, can cause us to possess nearly super-strength. There is a chemical, which produces a sedative-type effect that calms us down, when we become overly excited or experience extreme stress and fear. There are other endorphins that do other jobs as well. The point that I'm trying to make is that the brain has a highly sophisticated chemical balance, which controls our mind and body. When we experience a stimulus, physical or visual, the computer in the brain determines which and how much of these endorphins are produced to achieve the proper or desired response. Alcoholics/addicts have a malfunctioning computer, which screws up the regulatory process of endorphin production---sometimes causing us to get the wrong amount of the wrong one---at the wrong time. This process is vastly more complicated than is being presented here. It is not necessary for you to understand all of this from a medical viewpoint. Just try to understand the concept. The absence of, or the improper combination of these chemicals in the brain causes a **PROFOUND EMOTIONAL IMBALANCE**.

This imbalance either contributes to or causes many other types of mental and physical problems, because every bodily function we have is negatively affected by our fouled-up body chemistry. When we are drinking and/or using drugs, we are not attentive to how out-of-balance our bodies are because we are high or numbed-out most of the time---or experiencing the discomforts of not being high or numbed-out. The life-style we lived did not include a balanced diet, proper rest, and general health care maintenance. It is nothing short of a miracle that any of us survive it. Since we are not capable of stepping out of our own skin and objectively observing ourselves, we are generally not able to recognize how significantly our bodies and our behavior are deteriorating. The most recognizable symptom, to us, is our erratic, inconsistent, and unstable emotional state. We go from one extreme to the other. We are either zooming and on top of the world or we are down in the pits of despair and emotional crisis.

At first, there is no middle ground for us. Radical mood swings are common. The more we drink and/or use other drugs, the less our brain properly produces and regulates those **essential chemicals---endorphins**. This increases the body's need to have more alcohol and/or drugs to compensate for the lack of normal body chemistry. This is when we begin to have feelings of craving for our "drug of addiction". I won't say "drug of choice", because if you are reading this chances are you are making a choice to not use or planning to give this to someone who you care about in hopes that they will make a choice to get help. The sad and greatly misunderstood fact is that our body chemistry becomes so screwed up and it becomes accustomed to functioning with the artificial chemistry that we use.

We lose the ability to not use. Our bodies no longer function without something in it. Remember---this is NOT a moral issue. This is a physical illness, which is diagnosable and treatable!!!!

Besides a noticeable increase in the use of alcohol/ drugs, here are some recognizable symptoms of radically changing neuro-chemistry:

- When not high or using, the alcoholic/addict has no natural ability to remain emotionally stable or consistent in his/her behavior.

- They/we experience very radical mood swings.

- A constant inability to deal with stress or simple responsibilities.

- Frequent lying and/or exaggerations of experiences.

- Eating disorders and/or digestive problems may evolve.

- Respiratory problems may develop.

- Cardiovascular problems in one form or another may develop.

- Kidney and liver problems are common.

In general folks, all of our bodily functions begin to go to hell on us. Don't think, for one second, that you can *"party"* and not pay a price for it. Eventually, our addiction demands that we have something in our system---just to stop shaking and vomiting long enough to function a little. By this time, we have lost the choice to use or not use. We simply cannot *"not do it"*. The most crippling element we face is the psychological imprisonment that we begin to suffer. By now, we are in a *"be- damned, if you do and be-damned, if you don't"* situation. Alcoholics Anonymous[1] refers to this as "a hopeless state of mind and body". It is truly that to those who reach that point of mere existence.

The **abnormal** and the **vile** have, for us, become the **normal**. At this point of physical and mental deterioration we have, in most cases, existed in this state for such a painfully long time, that we have lost any concept of what life would be like without the drink and/or drugs. Our painfully, twisted emotional state now totally dictates what our actions will be. Now we simply *"use to exist"* and *"exist just to use"*. Common sense will tell you that any and all decisions, large or small, made while in this state are *NOT* trustworthy. The determining factor in our decision-making process, at this point, is solely to alleviate stress and pain. The physical pain we suffer is real and terrible, but the mental and emotional pain we suffer defies adequate description. The guilt and remorse we impose on ourselves is far more painful than the criticism and lack of understanding by family and friends.

GET BUSY!!!

Hopefully, by this point, something you have read, heard, or felt will spark a moment of clear thinking, which will motivate you to begin on a course of positive action in respect to your recovery or the recovery of the person you purchased this book for. You may be saying under your breath,

"Well, that's why I have my face in this book!"
"Good!!!!!"

Keep it here for a while. In fact, when you are through reading this, put it in the bathroom, near the toilet, so whenever you are sitting on the throne, you can pick this up and get your batteries recharged. Think this sounds stupid? Well, you probably have hugged the porcelain god, quite a bit over the years, so sitting on it to read really doesn't sound so strange---right? Plus, if you haven't stopped drinking/using yet, you can look at this book while you are barfing up your guts and **know** that you really don't have to feel this way anymore---**Not Ever!!!!!!** I've only vomited about four or five times in the last 17 years and that was due to the flu. That, alone, is a miracle for me! At one time, I could tell you the name of every major toilet manufacturer in the world. *I wonder why!* God, how wonderful it is not to have to live that way anymore! Neither do you or your loved ones!!

Chapter Five

VALUE SYSTEM

A Code of Conduct: Family, Church, School, Peer Relationships, Jobs, Civic Responsibilities, and Community Relations

Simplified Explanation: If we stay within the boundaries of our value system, we generally feel good about ourselves. If we deviate from our value system, we feel guilt and remorse, which for us usually results in our drinking/drugging. If we make amends for the violation of our value system, then we feel better about ourselves.

Recovery: We begin to reapply old values we had learned, *but put aside,* during our addiction/alcoholism. We also begin to learn new and sometimes more rigid values from those whom we associate with in recovery. By actively participating in a regular 12-step group, we become teachable, change, and grow spiritually. Eventually, we develop a reasonable value system and we learn how to function normally within that system.

Chapter Six

FOUR EASILY RECOGNIZABLE SYMPTOMS OF OUR DISEASE: ISOLATION, DENIAL, DELUSION, and CONFUSION

ISOLATION:

Eventually, we stop socializing with people who do not *"party"* like we do. We stop attending or participating in social functions, unless we know that it will be acceptable to drink and/or use drugs, while at the function. Most of us eventually deteriorate to the point of preferring to stay home and *"party"* alone. It seems that our booze and dope lasts longer that way and we don't have to worry about getting arrested. This also means that we can throw-up or pass-out without worrying about someone stealing our stash. Many of us develop feelings of paranoia, which is fueled by extreme fear. Although we are not always able to identify what we are afraid of, the fear and paranoia can be paralyzing.

If you can relate to this, in any way, stop for a moment and think about how this disease has made you a **prisoner of your own fears**. In most cases, the fear is of your own making and is usually unfounded. Even though the perceived threat may not be real, the fear is very real.

IT JUST DOESN'T HAVE TO BE THAT WAY---ANYMORE!!

Without realizing it, we have developed a frame of mind that causes us to either put people up on a pedestal, looking at them in an unrealistic way---or--

-we look down on them considering ourselves to be *"better than they are"*. Neither attitude is appropriate or wise.

We begin to break free of this problem, when we begin to see people eye-to-eye and perceive them, and ourselves, as neither greater nor lesser. We are all in the same process of growth, change, and development. Each person is in his/her own particular level of understanding; however, we are all in the same process.

DENIAL SYSTEM:

"I don't have a problem."

"I just like to party."

"I can handle it."

"I can stop anytime I want to."

"If everyone would just leave me alone, I would be just fine."

"If you had to put up with all the crap that I have to, you'd stay high too."

Does any of this sound familiar to you? It is very simple. If alcohol and drugs are contributing to the problems in our lives, then they **ARE** a problem! We cannot stop drinking by going on a reefer-maintenance program. Neither can we get off drugs by going on an alcohol-maintenance program. We become substance-free by not using **ANY KIND** of mood- altering substance. Our ego and false pride are major barriers to our sobriety. Sometimes it is difficult for us to accept the fact that we are not ten feet tall and bullet proof.

DELUSION:

A system of thinking that supports denial: "It isn't true, but it is logical." It is knowing things to be, that just aren't so. We are capable of justifying to ourselves **anything** we think, feel, do, or don't do. Our defense mechanisms are very sophisticated and well developed---so much so that we do not have the ability to recognize them in ourselves. It is difficult at first, to realize that there is, indeed, something wrong with our thinking. Some of our thinking is wrong, some is incomplete, and some of it is really warped. Our ego doesn't want to allow us the human element of error.

The first thing we must overcome is the notion that we can drink or use drugs successfully. The next thing we must accept is, that as human beings, we will periodically make judgment calls that are not as wise, as we first thought them to be. That is normal. I don't know any flawless people. Also, accepting the fact that we are dealing with a disease, as well as a way of thinking makes it easier to seek help.

Ask yourself this:

If you had cancer or diabetes, would you go to a doctor for help?

Of course you would! What we are dealing with here is no different. Neither is it any less destructive and deadly. Do **NOT** try to do recovery on your own. **GET HELP!!!**

CONFUSION:

Confusion is a normal state of mind at the beginning of recovery. At first, we ask ourselves too many questions like:

"How the hell did I get this way?"

"Who or what is the cause of all this?"

"Will the fear ever leave?"--- and so on and so on.

Not only do we ask ourselves too many questions in the beginning, but we actually hold ourselves responsible for having the answers to all those questions. **NO WAY!!!** All of those questions are normal, but there is no way you should expect yourself to be able to answer them, at this point in your recovery.

There is time to sort out all of those things and it will, indeed, take time to put the pieces of the puzzle back in order.

Right now, you aren't supposed to have all the answers!

You are simply responsible for having a **little WILLINGNESS** to be shown what the answers are. Those answers will come to you a-little-at-a-time throughout the **PROCESS** of recovery. If you are willing to do the footwork, there are many people available to help you along your way. **IF** you are not willing to go to **ANY LENGTH** to be clean and sober---and stay that way, then you don't want it bad enough to make it.

YOU ARE RESPONSIBLE FOR YOUR OWN RECOVERY!!!

Recovery is not for people who need it. It is for people who WANT it bad enough to follow directions and take suggestions----WHETHER YOU LIKE IT OR NOT!!

There will plenty of times, when you won't like some of the things that are suggested. If it were painless and fun all the time, the success ratio would be much higher than it is. So what it all boils down to is *"GET REAL—OR DIE!"*

Confusion is not always a negative state of mind. Most of the time, when we are experiencing confusion, it is because we are reevaluating our situation and are seeking a better solution. That, alone, indicates that we are not locked into an unchangeable mindset. For us to recover, we must always remain open-minded and willing to change and grow in areas of our thinking. So in most cases, confusion is just a state of reassessment of *"where we are"*, *"what we think and feel"*, and *where we are headed"*. All of this is necessary for continued progress in recovery and spiritual growth, which maintains our sobriety.

Chapter Seven

OUR GREATEST STUMBLING BLOCKS: FALSE PRIDE and EGO

This can be easily illustrated by using a bicycle wheel as an analogy: Let the spokes of the wheel represent all of the different variables of our lives, such as job, family, community responsibilities, boss, co-workers, people, places, and things. *WE were the axle,* meaning that we orchestrated our lives, such that all of the variables revolved around us and *what* we wanted, the *way* we wanted, and *when* we wanted it. We manipulated everything and everyone in our lives to accommodate what *we* thought, felt, believed, and wanted. We manipulated people and situations to suit our own life-style, in a manner that is unchallenging to where we are and what we want or don't want. Our whole universe revolved around us, like a wheel revolves around an axle.

In sobriety and reality, we begin to learn that our real place, in the scheme of things, is to *become one of the spokes.* We learn how to:

let GOD become the axle.

We learn how to become *a part of*---instead of---*the center of.* We are no greater than nor less than those around us.

Chapter Eight

EXAMINING OLD BEHAVIOR

DIFFERENT INTENTIONS
+<u>SAME OLD BEHAVIOR</u>
SAME UNSUCCESSFUL RESULTS

Different Intentions, which never materialize...

How many times have we said,

"I'll never do that again!" or *"It will be different this time."*

How many times while being hung-over or strung-out, have we thought,

"God, if you get me through this, I'll never do it again!"

How many times have we said those same things to our family members, friends, employers, God, and anyone else who would listen? I can remember making all of those promises, many times, with **honest intentions** of keeping them. I vividly remember wanting to quit, swearing to quit, and really intending to quit. I did not realize that I had a **DISEASE that GUARANTEED** that I would repeat the same old behavior.

SAME OLD BEHAVIOR

The same old behavior is the result of using under-developed and inappropriate social and survival skills. The life-style we developed, while drinking and/or using drugs, stops the development of these skills. We begin to use only those social and communicative skills that are required to function in our immediate environment, which itself begins to shrink, as we continue to drink and drug. We venture out less, interact with others less, especially with those who don't drink or drug the way we do. We progressively stop participating in things that challenge us physically and mentally. Many of the social and communicative skills that we learned are forgotten or distorted to conform to what has become an inappropriate and destructive life-style. We slowly begin to lose touch with reality, as it is.

REALITY becomes the ENVIRONMENT, as we PERCEIVE it to be, when we are high.

The abnormal becomes the normal. We lose sight of the fact that there is another way to live. We place great value on things that are only temporary and lose sight of the great value of those things, which are permanent.

Things of man decay and wither. Things of GOD are permanent.

SAME UNSUCCESSFUL RESULTS

Although we may believe that we are doing the best we can with what we have to work with, the results increasingly become **FRUSTRATION, TROUBLE, and MISERY.**

If we continue doing what we are doing, We will continue getting what we are getting. If I want my life to be different, then I must be willing to do things differently.

Chapter Nine

FORMULA FOR CHANGE: ATTITUDE = BEHAVIOR = LIFE'S CIRCUMSTANCES

Our initial focus must be on realizing the necessity of developing and maintaining an open mind about examining new information and reexamining what we think, feel, and believe. This is the beginning of becoming **teachable**.

There are many things about our lives that we are powerless to change. However, no matter how messed up things become, we can still control our attitude.

Think about it a moment!

Circumstances dictate much of what goes on in our lives, but how we deal with those circumstances is **OUR CHOICE**. We **choose** our attitude.

All difficult or painful situations have something positive to offer us, **if we simply look for it**. We are usually not able to see the positive, when we are in the middle of dealing with the situation. However, after using our support system to help us get through the situation, we can look back on it and learn a great deal from having persevered through the difficulty. Like the old saying goes,

"What doesn't kill us will make us stronger."

To help maintain a positive attitude toward any situation, ask yourself a couple of simple questions and answer them **HONESTLY!!**

1. What *"can I do"* or *"not do"*, *"say"* or *"not say"* to contribute to a harmonious solution to the situation? Once you have identified what you *"can do"*, no matter how small or insignificant it may seem, you must ask yourself the second question.

2. *Am I willing to take this action?*

3. *"If I'm not willing to take this action, then can I accept the situation, as it is, and be okay anyway?*

By going through the self-questioning process, we begin to learn that not only are we responsible for our own attitude, but there is much we can do to control our attitude.

Our **BEHAVIOR** will always reflect what our attitude is. A positive attitude will produce positive results and more appropriate behavior. A negative attitude will produce negative, pessimistic, and inappropriate behavior. The circumstances of our lives are determined by our behavior.

Being aware of all of this doesn't mean that we are instantly capable of maintaining a positive attitude---all of the time. Like any other good habit, it takes a lot of time and effort to *condition ourselves to LOOK FOR THE POSITIVE!!*

A great deal of our emotional stability and ability to remain calm depends on our neuro-chemistry. Once entering into recovery, our body chemistry will require the better part of three years to repair itself to normal balance. We must be able to change our attitudes and behavior **L O N G *before*** our body is ready to facilitate this. This is why a support group and a sponsor or mentor is so necessary. We generally do not do change very gracefully. The encouragement and support of others, who have succeeded, plays a major role in our success.

Chapter Ten

THREE DANGEROUS FEELINGS THAT WE MUST DEAL WITH QUICKLY: FEAR, RESENTMENT, and ANGER

FEAR:

Fear is the root of most of our difficulties.

"Fear of not acquiring what we feel we need or must have, in order to be okay or content."

"This may be the fear of not being loved the way we feel we need to be."

"It could be the fear of not succeeding in our jobs or professions the way we feel that we should."

"It could be the fear of not being as good a husband or wife as we would like to be."

"It could be the fear of not being as good a parent as we would like to be."

"Fear of losing what we have already acquired, such as success, love, health, opportunities, relationships, etcetera."

MOST OF OUR FEARS STEM FROM UNREALISTIC EXPECTATIONS OF OTHERS AND OURSELVES.

RESENTMENT:

Resentments are usually the result of blaming others or situations for our state of affairs. Recovering people cannot afford to hold onto resentments, because we get high or drunk over them. For us,

There is no such thing as JUSTIFIABLE ANGER, IF we plan to stay clean and sober.

As mentioned earlier, our attitude will determine how we deal with these feelings.

The 12-step programs and other support groups, teach us how to deal with old resentments, as well as how to avoid developing new resentments.

The subject of resentments should not be taken lightly.

RESENTMENTS are the NUMBER ONE CAUSE of RELAPSE!

It takes a while, in recovery, to learn how to deal with resentments appropriately, without feeling the need to drink or drug.

ANGER:

This is an OUTWARD manifestation of the INWARD feeling of fear. Look at it truthfully! If you are angry with someone, something, or situation right now, it is because---in some way---you feel *THREATENED!!!* The threat we perceive may be monetary, physical, sexual (threat to ego), or some kind of threat to our overall security. For many of us, the feeling of anger is a gift, because before recovery we never felt anger. We went from *PISSED OFF straight to RAGE!!!* A state of anger simply suggests that we are extremely discontent and we are thinking it or inwardly stewing about it. Rage is when we act on those feelings in an uncontrolled manner. Rage is usually destructive and spontaneous. Our rage usually compounds our problems. It is okay to feel angry about something. What's important is that we learn how to deal with the anger, without inappropriate behavior.   It is only a feeling. *Feelings change*.   We need to learn how to allow a cooling-off period, before acting on any form of anger.

One of the benefits of recovery is that we learn to process the anger, without making others victims of our anger.   We learn how to **RESPOND** instead of **REACT** to the situation.   Reaction is immediate, impulsive behavior, based purely on emotions---which are quite upset---*at that moment!* To respond, we allow a cooling-off period to think about the situation, **BEFORE** we take action.   We need to process *what we think about the situation*, as well as *what we feel about the situation*. The difficult thing in this process is to be as objective as possible looking at what *our part* in the situation *really* was.

If I'm angry at a person, place or situation, somewhere along the way, I played a part in the creation of the situation. Most of the time, the absolute truth is painful, because I am faced with *my part in it!!* This is hard to do, even if you have allowed a cooling-off period. It is virtually impossible, if you haven't.

In recovery, we learn many ways of defusing anger. One of the most effective ways is to call our sponsor or someone else in our support group. The purpose for this is to allow us an opportunity to blow off steam, vent our feelings, and get another person's unbiased viewpoint. A third party has a degree of objectivity that we don't have, because they stand to neither gain nor lose anything by expressing their honest opinion.

A real friend will tell you the truth, not necessarily what you want to hear.

We all feel anger at times, but part of changing and growing is learning how to effectively and appropriately respond to the situation, instead of reacting to it. This is not something that automatically occurs, just because we are now aware of it. This takes much practice on a daily basis, but it does happen. After some time practicing this, we find ourselves spontaneously responding differently to situations that *used to trip our trigger!*

Keep in mind that the material presented in this book takes time, great effort, and constant practice to apply these principles and tools to our lives. Needless to say, the more we practice, the better we become at applying these principles and the more normal they begin to feel to us. The contents of this book, are by no means the solution to all of your problems; however in these pages, you will find a:

Beginning point and an overview of some of the key elements and tools of sober living.

Chapter Eleven

OUR BASIC TOOLS OF CHANGE: HONESTY, OPEN-MINDEDNESS, and WILLINGNESS

HONESTY:

At first, our emotions are so battered that we are not capable of being as honest with ourselves, as we will be later in our recovery. We must first be as honest as we can be with *"others"* and *"ourselves"*. Then, we learn the importance of being *completely* honest in *ALL* of our affairs.

Honesty, with ourselves, begins with realizing that we can no longer socially or recreationally drink or use drugs successfully. By now, the consequences of our behavior are beginning to get our attention, as well as the attention of others around us. Family members and friends recognize the seriousness of our problem, before we do. Unfortunately, we don't pay much attention to the comments or suggestions that are made, in regard to our getting help.

Very frequently, friends and/or family members want to help, but do not know what to do or say to motivate us to take a good look at ourselves and our destructive, hurtful behavior. You may very well have received this book from such a person, who truly cares about you and this is their way of trying to show you their concern.

Once we have been able to admit to ourselves that we have a problem, that *WE REALLY CANNOT CONTROL*, we begin to seek help. Unfortunately, for those who are very hardheaded and closed-minded, hitting that bottom may include total financial ruin, loss of health, prisons, and other types of institutions---even death. Our ability to continue being honest, in all things will increase, as we remain clean and sober.

OPEN-MINDEDNESS:

We begin to realize that, for a long time, we have made a wide variety of excuses for our drinking and drug use.   We blamed others and our drinking, drugging, and for our deviant behavior. At this point, we begin to learn that:

OUR THINKING IS THE "REAL CULPRIT".

Realizing this, we begin the process of recovery, which allows us to change, *a little at a time*. We also begin to systematically examine our thinking and learn how to change it, progressively. We must always remain receptive to new and better input.

Example: A mechanic has to rebuild an automobile engine. All he has to work with is an old toolbox he has had forever, with tools that are old, rusty, and half-worn out. Then someone brings him a new huge toolbox with a variety of new tools and wrenches, a compressor, and a large assortment of sockets and pneumatic tools. Some of these tools are things he has never seen before. But now he has someone right there to explain what each of the new tools are and then teach him how to use each one proficiently!!!

The point is that he can struggle with old, worn out tools, skinning his knuckles, pulling muscles, wrestling with frustration, and spending a great deal of time getting the job done---**OR**---he/she can use new, more effective tools, which will allow him/her to complete the job in less time with less strain or personal injury, less frustration, and much more efficiency.

Common sense shows us, which is the better way to go!

Although difficult at first, if we continue trying, our open-mindedness will improve. As it improves, we begin to learn more about recovery and become better able to apply what we learn. If we take an honest look at how we acquired all of our knowledge, we realize that someone taught us everything we know. For the most part, they were teachers, professors, coaches, pastors, friends, co-workers, and supervisors.

Recovery is no different!

At some point in time, we come to realize that we must allow others to teach us how to stop using alcohol and drugs and ***STAY STOPPED!*** Then we learn to live life differently, normally, and happily from the same people---those who have been where we have been and survived it to move on in life. We must become teachable and stay that way.

WILLINGNESS:

1. To fearlessly examine ourselves.

2. To become teachable.

3. To examine and try new concepts.

4. To participate in an established community support system.

5. To develop and use a personal support system.

6. To help other newcomers learn to do the same things that you have been taught to do in order to achieve sobriety.

WILLINGNESS TO EXAMINE OURSELVES FEARLESSLY

ARE YOU CHEMICALLY DEPENDENT?

1. Do you drink or use drugs to reduce nervousness?

2. Do you require a drink or drug in the morning, in order to function?

3. Do you prefer to drink/drug alone?

4. Do you lose time from work due to hangovers or "burnout"?

5. Does you're "partying" create problems at home?

6. Does your drinking/using make you careless with your family's welfare?

7. Do you feel craving for a drink or drug during the day?

8. Do you feel irritable, when you are not high?

9. Has drinking or using changed your personality?

10. Do you have difficulty sleeping?

11. Has drinking/drugging made you more impulsive?

12. Have you noticed a decrease in your initiative and ambition?

13. Are decisions easier to make after having a few drinks or getting a buzz?

14. Do you drink/use to feel at ease during social functions?

15. Do you feel more secure when you have a buzz?

16. When not drinking, do you have feelings of inadequacy?

17. Are you jealous or super-protective of your significant other?

18. Do you have erratic mood swings?

19. Has your efficiency decreased since drinking/drugging?

20. Are you harder to get along with when not drinking or buzzing?

21. Are you spending more time in less wholesome environments?

22. Has your health experienced any significant change?

23. Do you always drink more than two drinks?

24. Do you use more medication than has been prescribed?

25. Do you ever have feelings of self-disgust?

If you have answered **YES** to three or more of these, then chances are you are one of us, ***and blessed to know it, while you are STILL breathing.***

Chapter Twelve

DENIAL: "I DON'T HAVE A PROBLEM".

SIMPLE DENIAL, MINIMIZING, RATIONALIZING and JUSTIFYING, INTELLECTUALIZING, DIVERSION or SHIFTING, and ANGER

SIMPLE DENIAL:

Absolute refusal to acknowledge that a problem exists.

MINIMIZING:

"I don't have a problem."

"I just like to party a lot!"

At first, we do not have the ability to realize how serious our problem is.

RATIONALIZING and JUSTIFIFYING:

"I work hard, so I deserve to play hard."

"Everybody else does it, so it's no big deal!"

Guess what? Everybody else **DOESN'T** do it and it **CAN** be a very big deal when we begin to have problems, as a direct result of our drinking and/or drugging.

"The world sucks anyway and this helps me put up with it!!!"

I've said those words in the past. I learned that when I stopped doing the things that made it *"suck"*, my world changed greatly for the *better!!!*

INTELLECTUALIZING:

If you can pronounce this, then you already have an idea of what it refers to. It took eleven years, going to four different colleges, pursuing three different majors, to come to the brilliant state of awareness I reached, when I found recovery.

> *My education and life experience was NOT sufficient to keep me from becoming a "knee-wobbling, toilet-hugging DRUNK and JUNKIE!!!*

I have worked in professional environments where social drinking and drugging were common and, at times, expected. If I had possessed the ability to see ahead to where it was going to take me and what it was going to put me through, you can bet your life that I would have done things differently.

Throughout my drinking and drugging career, I was able to manipulate people and situations to accommodate my self-centered thinking. By the time I hit my bottom, I had used, conned, manipulated, and screwed myself into a hopeless state of mind and body. My great wisdom and experience only allowed me to prolong my misery.

Oh how fortunate are those whose drinking and drugging takes them to a bottom in just a few short years. They are able to turn their lives around and spend the majority of it in relatively productive contentment. Some grow to enjoy great success and real joy in their lives.

DIVERSION or SHIFTING:

Many times, when confronted about our drinking or using, we make unsuccessful attempts to divert the problem. Many times, we will develop other addictions, while trying to stop one.

I remember a period of time that I stopped drinking, for eleven months, but the amount of marijuana that I smoked and the amount of speed that I took DOUBLED! I was not in any kind of recovery program at the time. I was just trying to control what I believed to be the problem, which was alcohol. I soon came to realize that I had an equally serious problem with drugs. Eventually, my addiction progressed to the point that I would use whatever drug was available, as well as alcohol.

When making attempts to stop or control my drinking, I would frequently substitute other things like food, sex, gambling, or any other type of "quick fix" that would alter the way I felt. We are quick to divert the focus on anything other than the real problem, which was our thinking and the way we felt about ourselves.

BLAMING OTHERS:

I was thoroughly convinced that my wife was the reason I drank like I did. I gave no thought to the fact that anyone who lived with a nut like me, for twenty years, would have to suffer from their own emotional problems. This is truly a family disease. Although some family members may not drink or use drugs, they are affected by the constant, inconsistent, and abusive behavior we impose upon them.

During the years of my drinking and drugging, I progressively became an unpredictable Jeckyl and Hyde type personality. The disease took away my ability to be a loving husband and father. I became a tyrant and a dictator who controlled every move my wife and children made. The worse I got, the more she withdrew into a shell of isolation. Our communication deteriorated to nothing. We eventually became like strangers living in the same house, just tolerating each other for the sake of our three daughters. I blamed her, jobs, and others for my miserable state of affairs. In my mind, drugs and alcohol were not the problem. They were my solutions to the problems.

I eventually ran out of excuses and realized that alcohol and drugs were destroying every aspect of my life and the lives of my family. I needed help, of some kind, but did not have a clue about where to start. I wasn't really sure about wanting to quit, but I was certain that I wanted my life to be different than what it had become. Blaming others only justified, to my sick mind, why it was okay to keep doing what I was doing. Total confusion and desperation had taken me to jail a few times and hospitals more time than I can count. I wrecked nine motorcycles in a ten-year span of time, totaling three of them.

I've been wired back together, quite a few times. The sad part about all of that was that I thought those types of things were normal aspects of the life-style that I lived. Living on the edge all of my life, I had just adapted to the fact that everyday could be my last, so I lived it wide open. I remember once buying a bass boat on a Thursday, insuring it on Friday, and wrecking it on Saturday. I hit three piers going about 55 miles per hour. It cost me a small fortune to repair the damaged property, not to mention tearing my boat all to hell. And yes, I was snockered, when it happened. Oh well! I thought that this was just not a good day. At the time, I never considered that I was powerless over alcohol and that my life had become unmanageable. Of course, I had a million excuses for why the accident occurred.

On the 14th of December 1987, I walked through the doors of a local treatment center and began a new life.

I was one of the *"educational variety"*. I had this *"determined need to understand why"* I was not capable of stopping and staying stopped. I met some wonderful and caring people who began educating me about this disease. The more I learned, the more I began to realize that my life had become the victim of my very distorted thinking.

Treatment opened the door to self-examination and self-confrontation. This was **NO FUN!!!** I immediately began attending Alcoholics Anonymous meetings, while going through treatment. During the early months of recovery, all of my excuses were taken away along with a boatload of anger, rage, and guilt. I felt a tremendous sense of freedom, when I found out that I had a diagnosable illness that could be arrested. I realized that I was not a bad guy, trying to be a good guy. I was a very sick man, trying to get well.

ANGER:

Who enjoys being wrong?

Who enjoys making bad decisions and having to deal with *the consequences?*

Who enjoys finding out that all of their life their concept of God was very distorted and incomplete?

Who enjoys coming face to face with their own character defects, realizing that those character defects have kept the sober and sane person trapped inside a drunk's and a junkie's body?

Who cares to admit utter defeat?

Who wants to admit that they had lost the ability to function normally in society?

Who wants to see the embarrassment and shame in the faces of our children when their friends come over to visit?

Not me—do you? Can you? Ultimately, **WILL YOU?**

This thoroughly pisses you off, doesn't it? That is probably because you have the "good fortune" of being one of "us", who have been blessed with the awareness of our malady and, by God's grace, are being given an opportunity to correct the problem---BEFORE IT IS TOO LATE!!!

I don't mind telling you that I was angry for a long time after coming into recovery. I had done a lot of damage to myself and other people---for a very long time. Needless to say, my life was a screwed-up mess. Feeling the anger was a necessary part of the healing process. First, I had to learn that it was okay to feel anger, even if I didn't know exactly what, why, or with whom I was angry. Then, I learned that I could feel anger, without letting it go to the point of rage.

I also learned that anger did not require retaliation or any other kind of physical response. In recovery, we learn many different ways to defuse our anger until we can identify and appropriately deal with its source. Keep in mind that:

Recovery is a process that teaches us all we have to know about dealing with the many different attitudes and feelings that surface as we move forward in our new life.

Identifying and learning how to properly deal with ourfeelings and attitudes is not an easy process. However, it is easier than living with them---the way we had been in the past. Anger is basically *an OUTWARD manifestation of the INWARD feeling of FEAR.*

Fear is not always bad. I have a healthy fear of what would happen if I picked up *JUST ONE* beer or smoked *JUST ONE* joint. In recovery, we learn to feel the fear or anger without allowing it to dictate our behavior. I used to think that courage was the absence of fear. I have since learned that:

Courage is the willingness to do the next right thing, even though I may be petrified with fear.

As we remain sober and become an active part of our recovering community, fear progressively plays less of a role in our lives. With sobriety comes spiritual maturity, which allows our faith to displace and replace fear, whenever it surfaces. We also begin to stop doing the things that set the stage for fear to enter in. We also live the 12 steps of recovery, which one step at a time---one day at a time, allows us to learn how to live a life that is relatively and reasonably happy, joyous, and free.

Learning to let go of the old people, places, and old behavior is difficult, but necessary. We must learn to have faith in the recovery **PROCESS**.

LETTING GO:

To "let go" does not mean to stop caring. It means I can't do it for someone else.

To "let go" is not to cut myself off, it is to realize that I cannot control another.

To "let go" is not to enable, but to allow learning from natural consequences.

To "let go" is to admit powerlessness, which means the outcome is not in my hands.

To "let go" is not to try to change or blame another, it is to make the most of myself.

To "let go" is not to care for, but to care about.

To "let go" is not to fix, but to be supportive.

To "let go" is not to judge, but to allow another to be a human being.

To "let go" is not to be in the middle of arranging all of the outcomes, but allow others to affect their own destinies.

To "let go" is not to be protective. It's to let another face reality.

To "let go" is not to deny, but to accept.

To "let go" is not to nag, scold, or argue, but instead to search out my own shortcomings and correct them.

To "let go" is not to adjust everything to my desires, but to take each day as it comes.

To "let go" is not to regret the past, but to grow from it and live in today.

To "let go" is to fear less and love more.

Chapter Thirteen

REALITY CHECK

What are my individual needs, desires, likes, and dislikes?

Are they reasonable?

Are they attainable with the skills I now possess---or do I need to further my education and job skills?

Does my life-style contribute to or detract from achieving and accomplishing my goals and desires?

Does alcohol and/or drugs keep telling me *'some day'* but *'some day'* never comes?

Do I have unrealistic expectations of others and myself?

Alcoholism and drug addiction **DEMANDS** that I become the center of my universe! Everything we think, feel, say, and do revolves around **SELF**.

Am I so focused on meeting my needs that I no longer contribute to my family and community, as I could and should?

Recovery allows us to make a more honest assessment of who, what, and where we actually are. Our close friends, whom we meet in our new recovering community, help us take an honest, hard, and painful look at ourselves. We need the objectivity of others to see those things in ourselves that we are unable to see. Honest, self-confrontation **MUST** occur before we can begin to experience permanent change in our lives. A support system, of some kind, is essential for alcoholics and addicts to maintain long-term sobriety.

Self-sufficiency DOES NOT WORK!!!!

In the beginning, we must abandon the idea that we can orchestrate our own recovery.

Chapter Fourteen

CRISIS MANAGEMENT: REACTING vs. RESPONDING

During active addiction, as well as the early months of recovery, we are prone to **REACT** to situations, instead of **RESPONDING** to them. Also, during this same time frame, our emotional state is very delicate and fragile. Our behavior has a tendency to be extreme, in that we under-react or over-react to most situations. This is the result of our emotional deterioration, due to extensive use of alcohol and/or drugs. Remember, as we discussed earlier, our decision-making processes are controlled by our emotions, which are battered and very reactionary.

What we begin to discover, in recovery, is how to **RESPOND** to situations instead of **REACTING** to them. We generally think of a reaction as an impulsive, instantaneous, and uncalculated response to a stimulus. When we respond appropriately, we take some time to think it through, weighing the pros and cons. Then we make a decision, based upon some type of process of evaluation. A response is also less likely to compound the situation or hurt someone. Learning how to respond to things takes some time and practice. It is part of the **PROCESS** of recovery. The longer we remain clean and sober, the more we change and become more proficient at responding appropriately to different situations, which used to trip our trigger.

UNREALISTIC EXPECTATIONS:

Most of us, during active addiction and early recovery, have had unrealistic expectations of others and ourselves. We expected a degree of perfection from others that they were not capable of living up to. We seldom gave thought to the human difficulties and daily sufferings of others, which prevent them from functioning in a state of flawlessness. Our self-centered thinking prevented us from seeing the human frailty of those around us. Again, the process of recovery allows us to begin to accept others and ourselves, just as we are, until changes begin to occur.

We come to understand that in the overall picture, we are no greater than nor less than anyone else. We are all in a process of spiritual growth and change, and for the most part, we are merely in different stages of our individual development.

When confronted with a situation that I find unacceptable to me, I now ask myself the following questions:

1. *What can I "say" or "not say"----"do" or "not do" to contribute to a harmonious solution to the situation?*

2. Am I willing or unwilling to take the appropriate action *defined in question #1?*

3. If I'm not willing to take that action, am I able to readjust my attitude and accept things just as the are for now?

Somewhere in those three questions, we will find the solution to any situation we may encounter. Keep in mind that our expectations were usually unrealistic. Because of those unrealistic expectations, we set ourselves up for disappointment---time after time. For us, disappointment usually results in anger or frustration or both, which usually resulted in our drinking or drugging. It is great to plan, but it is essential for us to remain open-minded and flexible, in respect to the outcome of our plans.

When leaving a place, headed for a specific destination, we become so focused on what is going to happen when we arrive; we completely miss the joy and growth of the journey itself.

Instead of living for the outcome, we should aspire to accomplish and learn to fully appreciate the process. After all, isn't that what life is---a journey? We come to understand and accept that the journey includes struggles, pain, and difficulties.

That's life; however, misery is optional.

Misery is an attitude that we do not have to adopt. You will hear this many times throughout your recovery:

Pain is necessary, but misery is OPTIONAL!

Chapter Fifteen

DEVELOPMENT OF A NEW AND POSITIVE LIFESTYLE

I had lived a dysfunctional life-style for so long that I began to believe that this life-style was normal. I believed that others, who did not drink or use drugs, were the exceptions to the norm. I had lost sight of the fact that there was another way of living, of which I had little or no knowledge.

A NEW LIFE-STYLE BEGINS WITH IMPROVING OUR GENERAL WELL-BEING.

H. A. L. T.:   Don't Get Too Hungry, Angry, Lonely, or Tired

H - HUNGRY:

Do not allow yourself to get too hungry. Usually, we are not very concerned with regular and healthy eating habits, when we are in active addiction and early recovery. Just remember to keep something in your stomach! After you have been sober a little while, you will be able to discipline yourself to eat a more regular and balanced diet.

A - ANGRY:

Do not react to anger. This is easier said than done, especially in early recovery. *PRACTICE* allowing yourself a cooling-off period, in order to *RESPOND* sensibly to whatever angers you.

Anger is not necessarily a bad feeling. It's how we handle it that determines whether it is bad or good. Many of us have good reason to be angry; however, few of us know how to process that feeling appropriately, in early recovery. We learn constructive ways of defusing the anger. It is definitely not a good idea to stuff it or bottle it up inside. Stuffing anger usually leads to an eventual explosion of **R-A-G-E,** which compounds our problems. The recovery process teaches us how to deal with anger appropriately.

L - LONELY:

When you attempt recovery alone, you are with your own worst enemy—*"your own thinking"*. We do not possess the ability to be totally objective about our thoughts and behavior. Use your support system that begins to develop immediately upon entering the recovery process.

First: Pray.

Second: Call someone in your support system.

Third: Go to a meeting.

Fourth: Try to help someone during the day.

Fifth: Pick up that 500-pound phone and call someone in your support group. It is essential that you get a list of names and phone numbers, during your early exposure to recovery.

Sixth: At the end of the day, take an inventory of your behavior throughout that day---to identify anywhere you may have offended anyone or acted-out on old behavior. Before going to sleep, pray again. This is a formula that will pretty-much keep you clean and sober----if you discipline yourself to do these things, without fail, every day. Of course, in this formula, is the premise that you do not drink or use during this day. *JUST DO IT!!!!*

T - TIRED:

Force yourself to slow down your pace and get adequate rest. Being tired and trying to function prevents us from accomplishing as much, as if we were rested. Fatigue also negatively affects the quality of our efforts, makes us moody, irritable, and discontent.

It is normal for us to experience two types of sleep dysfunction during early recovery. It is also temporary and will pass in time. This is really nothing more than your body chemistry getting back to a normal production of endorphins.

Here is what you can expect to occur with your sleep patterns is very early recovery:

1. *CANNOT GET TO SLEEP:* You may have worked all day and had a busy evening. You are feeling very tired and worn out. But, when you lie down, your eyes won't shut and your mind is going a thousand miles per hour. You cannot get your mind to shut down---no matter how tired you are.

2. *WANT TO SLEEP ALL OF THE TIME:* This too, is just another process of your body chemistry readjusting. This is *NOT* abnormal. If this state continues for a prolonged period of time, it may be a sign of clinical depression and should be treated by a physician. However, do not be too quick to diagnose yourself as suffering from clinical depression, when you are in the early months of recovery.

Our body and mind goes through many different types of changes, when we remain abstinent from drugs and alcohol. It takes a while for our bodies to readjust to a state of normal that we have not experienced for a long time, if ever. Give your body sufficient time to make this adjustment before becoming alarmed about possible depression.

Lets' face it, we have just given up our best friends, booze and dope, which always got us through the hard times, made us feel better when we were frightened or angry, and gave us courage when we had none. It had become our friend, our lover, and our life, and at the end---***our enemy.*** It is only natural that we go through a period of feeling depressed, sad, angry, and confused at now having to learn how to deal with life without this "old friend".

Chapter Sixteen

DEVELOP A WRITTEN PLAN FOR YOUR RECOVERY

Get a spiral-ring notebook and use it this way:

1. Write **PRAY.** If you don't know how to pray, then asksomeone to teach you. Your prayer-life will improve over time, but *it is the most effective and powerful tool* that you have.

2. Write H. A.L.T.. Do not let yourself get too hungry, angry, lonely, or tired.

3. Make or pick up a list of the 12-Step meetings in your area, specifically Alcoholics Anonymous (AA) and Narcotics Anonymous (NA). Then, commit to attend as many meetings as you can during your first ninety (90) days of sobriety. Attending meetings, at first may feel awkward, but that will quickly pass. You will begin to feel happy about being a part of a fellowship of people who share the same problems and who are there to help each other recover.

There are two times when you should attend a meeting:

When you feel like you need a meeting.
And
When you feel like you DON'T need a meeting.

It isn't likely that, at your first reading, you will understand the true value of everything in this publication. *JUST DO IT!!!* You will 'come to understand' the wisdom of each tool and exercise I have suggested.

Learning to live life sober requires exercise in doing things that may seem foreign or even stupid to us, at first:

1. ***Get a 12-step sponsor and use that person.*** Make yourself call this person frequently--- ***DAILY, if necessary.*** If you do not know what a sponsor is, then go to an AA meeting and find out! ***REMEMBER:*** Although there are hundreds of people around you, who would be all to happy to work with you, ***it is YOUR responsibility to reach out to them.***

You must take the initiative to follow the suggestions of those who have 'been there, done that'. Try to remain as open-minded as possible.

YOU are responsible for your own recovery.

All the phone numbers, tools of recovery, and helpful people are ***NO GOOD TO YOU, UNLESS YOU USE THEM!!!!!***

2. ***Use part of your notebook to journal in.*** Simply go to a quiet place daily. Write in your journal what you are feeling and thinking, at that moment. This is not for anyone to read, but ***YOU!!*** The purpose is two-fold: First, it has great therapeutic value, because you are expressing things that you have been stuffing inside. There is something magical about writing down our feelings. Try it, you'll see!! Second, as the weeks and months pass, you can reflect back on your old writings and recognize tremendous change in your thinking and your life. I suggest you journal daily for a couple of years, if you are able to discipline yourself to do it that long. This is one of those things that you just have to try to see the value of it.

Using the tools of recovery that I am sharing with you, in this book, does not feel natural or normal, at first. They become natural and normal with just a little self-discipline and a lot of practice.

Chapter Seventeen

ATTITUDE + BEHAVIOR = LIFE'S CIRCUMSTANCES

If we remain open-minded, we will begin to develop a willingness to rearrange our attitude to be more *POSITIVE* in our thinking and in our actions. As the result, our *BEHAVIOR* will begin to reflect that positive thinking. We begin to *DO* more things that bring about *POSITIVE RESULTS*. As a *RESULT* of *MORE* positive behavior, our life's circumstances *IMPROVE*. When we stop using drugs and drinking, we also stop doing most of the things that caused us most our grief and difficulties. With the absence of much of the old madness and chaos, we begin to feel much better about ourselves. Relationships improve. Job performances improve. Actually, just about every aspect of our life begins to show gradual signs of improvement.

Not everyone in your recovering community has a positive attitude. Some people are there just to get the law of their butts or perhaps to keep their significant other off their back. You will encounter many people trying to get sober for many different reasons. Their attempts will usually fail, until they realize that each person, who is so blessed to make it to the rooms of recovery, must be there *FOR HIMSELF OR HERSELF!!!* Sobriety is a personal thing that can only be achieved by and for the person putting forth the effort. Without sobriety, our lives are destined for jails, prison, hospitals, institutions, or the morgue!!!!!

Without sobriety, we will eventually lose everything and everyone that we hold dear. In doing the 12-steps of recovery, you will come to understand how God gets personally involved in our recovery and is, *ultimately* the source of all healing and progress. You will *NEVER--EVER* have to feel the agony of loneliness that you may have felt in the past. You will *NEVER AGAIN* have to be paralyzed by fear, anxiety, or depression. *YOU CAN DO IT! BELIEVE IT AND KNOW IT!!!*

"EASY DOES IT!"

In the beginning, we *MUST* develop a new *ATTITUDE*. It is much too soon to expect that you should be able to right all the wrongs of your past. We come to realize that we have hurt many family members, friends, and business associates. However, relationships and hurt feelings will mend, in time. Anger will leave others, and us in time.

Begin by forgiving yourself and making a commitment to *YOURSELF* to slow down and smell the roses. No matter how difficult or tragic things may appear to be, we all can find things to be grateful for. It is those things and the feeling of gratitude, that we must always hold onto. *Remember, that recovery is a process and it takes time.* We did not get screwed up overnight. By the same token, we aren't going to get well overnight. We have been mentally conditioned to 'live on the edge', reacting spontaneously to everything around us. As we begin to change, we learn how to *RESPOND* to things, instead of *REACTING* to them. The ability to slow down and *stay in TODAY* will improve as time passes, if we remain sober.

There is a big difference between **ABSTINENCE** and **SOBRIETY**. Abstinence is not drinking or using, but being stuck in the same old behavior, which in turn, breeds the same old consequences.

SOBRIETY IS ABOUT CHANGE!!

The willingness to learn about the disease, tools of recovery, to allow people to teach you how to use those tools, to face our fears, and/or to use whatever faith we have and move forward. Anytime you are honestly trying and the outcome isn't what it should be, you have still succeeded at something: *You simply discovered something that doesn't work!* Stop thinking in terms of failing at something and think in terms of *discovery!* As we apply the principles and tools of recovery, we **DISCOVER** an entirely **NEW WORLD**. As we grow in early recovery, we are taught to recognize certain triggers, which could lead us to relapse.

RELAPSE is also a PROCESS and not an occurrence.

Our thinking and behavior starts to revert back to 'old thinking' and 'old behavior', before we actually use or drink. Relapse begins the very moment we **STOP** doing, *on a daily basis*, **ALL** of the things we were taught to get sober. Usually, prayer is the first thing that the person stops doing faithfully. Then, the person begins to cut back on meetings. Their behavior becomes increasingly irritable and defensive. Often, they will begin to isolate, especially avoiding those who are a part of his/her immediate support group. As you can see below, relapse has very identifiable symptoms:

1. I start to doubt my ability to stay sober.

2. I deny my fears.

3. I adamantly convince myself that "I'll never drink again".

4. I decide that being abstinent is all that I need.

5. I try to force sobriety on others.

6. I become over-confident or cocky about my recovery.

7. I avoid talking about my problems and my recovery.

8. I behave compulsively, going from one extreme to another.

9. I over-react to stressful situations.

10. I start isolating.

9. I become preoccupied with one area of my life.

10. I start having periods of depression.

11. I start making haphazard plans with unrealistic expectations of the outcome.

12. I live in the 'the past' instead of the 'here and now'.

13. I find that my plans are beginning to fail, usually because we are trying to stay in control of everything. (*Most of us are 'control-freaks' anyway!*)

14. I waste time with idle-daydreaming and wishful-thinking.

15. I view my problems as unsolvable---negative attitude.

16. I long for happiness, but don't have a clue of where to start.

17. I avoid trying to have fun.

18. I become overly analytical---of everything!!

19. I become irritable with family and friends.

20. I experience frequent periods of confusion.

21. I am easily angered.

22. I revert back to blaming others for my problems.

23. I forget just how cunning, baffling, powerful, and **patient** this disease really is---*gettingtoo comfortable—too quickly!!*

24. I get away from balanced meals and start **'eating on the run'**.

25. I have frequent periods of listlessness.

26. I stop allowing regular times for rest and sleep.

27. I progressively get away from a daily routine.

28. I sporadically attend AA/NA and/or Aftercare meetings.

29. I develop a 'don't care' attitude.

30. I obsess over money, sex, and power.

31. I openly reject offers of help.

32. I regress to thinking that drinking/drugging can't make my life any worse than it is. Early sobriety is difficult, because our lives don't get straightened out as quickly as we would like for them to. *Hang in there!*

33. I start getting the 'poor me's'---feeling sorry for myself.

34. I begin to have fantasies about 'partying'.

35. I begin to consciously lie about things.

36. I increase use of prescribed or over-the-counter medications.

37. I develop and hold onto resentments.

38. I begin to visit drinking/using friends and places.

39. I think I am cured.

40. I make major changes in my life.

41. I forget to be grateful. We must not forget how far we have come in our recovery.

Happiness is not 'having what you want', but 'wanting what you have'.

42. I start using a mood-altering substance that may not be My substance of choice (addiction), thinking it's *OKAY* because we are not using the 'stuff' that we had the problem with.

43. I try 'controlled' drinking/using.

44. I lose all-control over what I'm using and return to my 'drug of choice'.

Chapter Eighteen

IMPROVING SELF-ESTEEM

If you keep doing what you're doing, you will keep getting what you're getting.

If we want our lives to **BE** different, then we must **BECOME WILLING** to do things differently. As we learn more about recovery and the recovering community, we learn more ways of doing things that make us feel better about ourselves. We also begin to learn how to 'let go' of the guilt and remorse. These have, many times, been the cause of our pain---which, in turn, was why we drank and/or used.

We will become what we feed our minds!

Recovery requires **POSITIVE THINKING** followed by **POSITIVE ACTION**. We must always be on guard to maintain a **POSITIVE ATTITUDE**, as consistently as possible. At first this seems almost impossible; however, it gets a little easier with time and practice. I do not know anyone who can maintain a positive attitude twenty-four hours a day. We just work at it "one day at a time", realizing that some days are going to be better than others. In the beginning of recovery, we seem to be both excited and very happy---or in the pits of despair and emotional crisis. It feels as though there is no middle ground. This changes in a few months, as we begin to experience that middle ground, where it's **OKAY** just to be **OKAY!** After some time, tears, and a lot of work on your personal recovery, you will begin to experience some balance in your life.

Much of what you have learned, up to this point, takes months to fully comprehend and apply effectively. It takes years of **DAILY PRACTICE** for these things to become a natural part of our lives. So don't expect this publication, or any other for that matter, to **FIX YOU.** That is God's job. Our job is to learn how to eliminate the obstacles, in our lives, that prevent God from doing **what he can and will do** in our lives.

Just for the record:

GOD IS STILL IN THE MIRACLE BUSINESS!!!

Every alcoholic and addict that has recovered from a 'hopeless state of mind and body' is a living testament to that fact.

My sole purpose for producing this publication is to let you know, **EMPHATICALLY,** that as long as you are breathing, there is **HOPE!!** As long as you are willing to continue trying, victory over this disease is possible for **YOU!!!**

A REVIEW OF THE TOOLS FOR STAYING STRAIGHT:

1. **PRAY.**

2. Stay away from the **FIRST** drink or drug.

3. Stay active.

4. Use the Serenity Prayer.

5. Go to meetings.

6. Keep an open mind.

7. Be patient with yourself and others.

8. Do not test your willpower.

9. Talk about your feelings.

10. Say what is on your mind. Be direct.

11. Try to recognize your progress.

12. Try to recognize your limitations and stay within their boundaries.

13. Stay out of the **CONTROL MODE.**

14. Accept responsibility.

15. Be honest in **ALL** of your affairs.

16. Organize your time as much as possible.

17. Develop better eating habits.

18. Develop some belief in a higher power and work diligently to expand your spiritual life.

19. Learn to trust others, realizing that people are not flawless and will make errors in judgment, at times, just like everyone else does. Give yourself and others permission to be human.

20. Avoid complaining.

21. Take the risk to change.

22. Exercise.

23. Change old routines.

24. Find and **USE** a sponsor.

25. Get adequate rest.

26. Avoid isolation.

27. Share your pain with your support group.

28. Share your joy with your support group.

29. Avoid resentments.

30. Keep it simple.

31. Maintain your gratitude.

32. Admit when you are wrong.

33. Stay in 'today'---one day at a time.

34. Live and let live. Allow others to be where they are. Don't have expectation of others' behavior.

35. "Easy does it". Don't get in a hurry. You have the rest of your life to work on this.

36. Avoid self-pity.

37. Ask for help when you need it. It is **YOUR** responsibility to reach out to those in your immediate recovering community, who have 'been there---done that'.

38. **DO NOT** be judgmental of others. God is working with them, just like he is with you.

39. Make your sobriety **NUMBER ONE** at first. Later in recovery, God will occupy that place.

40. Try new things that bring you enjoyment--- wholesome things.

41. Always be willing to help another who reaches out for help.

Chapter Nineteen

WILLINGNESS, COMPLIANCE, and COMMITMENT

WILLINGNESS:

Willingness does not mean that you have to like or even understand the suggestions that are given to you by your support group and/or sponsor. It simply means: ***Do it anyway, because it is what's best for you---at that moment.*** It means to try to give it your best shot, in spite of your fears and/or what your old peers may say. Do not let your fears create excuses in your mind for not following through with your recovery. There are over nineteen million of us in the U.S.A. alone, who have been right where you are now and have succeeded in their recovery efforts. Faces, places, and names may be different, but the fears and the pain are the same for all of us. You can be assured of that: **IF *WE* CAN MAKE IT, YOU CAN TOO!!!!!!**

COMPLIANCE:

Compliance, in recovery, simply means that I may not like or agree with what I hear but, "I am willing to try what is suggested by those who have gone before me."

Alcohol and other drug addictions make no distinction in regards to race, gender, social stratification, or occupational placement in life. This disease cripples and kills very intelligent and talented people every day. This disease takes sensitive, talented, and caring people and turns us in to sociopaths and prisoners in our own skin. The disease takes away our ability to use our positive qualities, while it accentuates and adds to our negative attributes. For the most part, we abandon our spiritual and religious beliefs, losing sight of just how special we are in God's eyes. By trying to apply the tools of recovery, we begin to regain our dignity and self-respect. We come to understand that there is truly a place and purpose for us in this world---a **MEANINGFUL** place and purpose.

Trust me when I tell you this:

"Where you are RIGHT NOW, in terms of feelings, fears, doubt, confusion, and possibly desperation, is not where you will be six months from now."

Sobriety involves constant change, personal growth, and becoming **TEACHABLE,** in order that we may **BECOME USABLE** in a more meaningful way. Once we have gotten sober, it is our responsibility and obligation to help others achieve sobriety. Most things change for the better with time. Recovery requires consistent **EFFORT.** We must work as hard at recovering as we did 'partying' all of the time.

NO PAIN---NO GAIN!!!

For us, compliance is putting forth the required effort to get the desired results.

At this point, you may be saying to yourself,

"Easier said than done!"

This is true. It is easier said than done. At some point in our recovery, we've all said those exact words---as well as periodically throughout the years of our sobriety. Neither myself nor anyone else, who has recovered from a *hopeless state of mind and body,* will ever tell you that it is easy. Quite the contrary, it will be the most difficult task that you have ever accomplished. Early recovery is difficult, but the rewards are beyond your wildest dreams. We come to know a state of peace and contentment that is beyond our ability to imagine. This is the result of doing the things we are taught in recovery. Not to say that life doesn't continue to challenge us with difficulties, trying times, and sometimes tragedies. The recovering lifestyle teaches us to deal with our feelings, both good and bad, more appropriately and effectively. We come to know that with God's help and the help of our new recovering community, we are able to deal appropriately with any kind of difficulty or hardship without having to drink or use drugs to cope.

Perhaps you are saying:

> **"I don't use drugs or drink to deal with my problems. I just like to party.""**

Well friend, where do you think the rest of us started? Not one of us picked up the first drink and said, **"Gee, I think I would like to become an alcoholic!""** No one rolled his/her first joint with the intentions of becoming an addict.

It is true that most people who begin recovery have hit some kind of bottom. For some, the bottom requires physical, mental, financial, and/or spiritual devastation. For others, a couple of D.U.I.s, an angry wife, boss, or both is all that is necessary to get their attention---in a serious way. No matter how far down it takes us, there are always lower levels waiting for us, if we continue the life-style.

It is very important to realize that we are not really unique or different from others with chemical dependency problems. Our ego tells us that we are different; therefore, all of this recovery stuff doesn't apply to us. Some folks approach recovery trying to determine **which** of the tools they will use and how they will go about it. ***Those are the ones we eventually bury.*** If you are questioning whether or not you are an alcoholic/addict, there is one sure way you can find out. Go to a few 12-step meetings and *SIT QUIETLY AND LISTEN*. Not all those meetings are about a bunch of old fogies telling war stories or drunk-a-logues. Those kinds of meetings are also very important to let you know where you could end up, if you don't take positive action *NOW*. Not everything in the meetings is about the gloom and doom of alcoholism and addiction. Quite the contrary, a great deal of what is shared in meetings is about:

WHAT IT WAS LIKE, WHAT HAPPENED, AND WHAT IT IS LIKE NOW.

The message of hope and the verification of continued success, in living chemically free, is the primary purpose of those meetings. There will be much that you hear that you will be able to identify with or relate to. There will be some new information you will hear that you have not been exposed to *YET*. At first, our ego doesn't want us to admit that our lives were much like theirs. ***Somehow, we are different---Yeah right!!*** When you attend these meetings, listen to the message and listen for similarities in your life. Don't go in there looking for differences. Look for similarities. Some of the most profound messages are given to us by some of the least likely people. God uses us all, no matter how broken we are.

If you continue drinking/drugging, it's just a matter of time before those problems and tragedies begin occurring or re-occurring in your life:

Who ever got married, expecting to get a divorce?

Who ever had children, expecting someone else to raise them?

Who ever started a business, expecting it to go bankrupt?

Who ever said, "I love you." with the intention of putting that person in the hospital, due to losing their temper?

Who ever took a drink with the intention of going out and killing someone in an automobile accident?

Who ever said, "Amen." intending to turn his back on everything he/she held sacred?

How many of us have said, "It won't happen to me!" and it did?

The point I'm trying to make is:

Your YET is there, patiently waiting for YOU!!!

Take your recovery more seriously than anything you have ever attempted.

It must be the number one priority, above all things and all relationships, except your relationship with God.

At this point, let's take a look at some behavior that leads to relapse:

1. Arguing with your significant other or other family members.

2. Not eating regularly or not having a balanced diet.

3. Sleeping too much or too little.

4. Isolating. We will spend too much time in our own heads, when keeping to ourselves. For most of us, that is *a dangerous place*. We usually get mugged when we go there.

5. Not talking with other people. Most of us don't socialize well sober, until we have had some practice at it. There must be a beginning---somewhere.

6. Having too much free time on your hands. We need to stay busy in early recovery.

7. Having unrealistic expectations of yourself and others. Give time---time.

8. Daydreaming about the *'good old days'*. If the good old days were all that good, I wouldn't have written this and you wouldn't be reading it---right?

9. Not following your counselor or sponsor's suggestions.

10. Getting back into the 'control mode'---wanting to do this thing 'your way'. Our brilliance and best efforts got us in the position we found ourselves in upon entering recovery.

11. Cutting back on or stopping going to meetings.

12. Not speaking up for yourself. We had become accustomed to being the bad guy, for so long, that we never learned how be assertive---without being aggressive. This will come in time.

13. Being dishonest.

14. Cutting back on or stopping daily prayer.

These are just some of the many danger signals that you will learn to look out for, while beginning your new life in recovery. The best years of your life lie ahead!!!!!!!!!!!

COMMITMENT:

Our commitment to recovery usually comes after we have been in recovery for a while. Few people come into recovery with the realization that they are powerless over drugs and alcohol and that their lives have become unmanageable. I am not powerless over whether or not I put the substance in my body; however, once I drink or use drugs, I am powerless over my behavior, thereafter. After drinking and/or using, I cannot guarantee what I will do or where I will end up. Once started, I am powerless to stop until I'm locked up, passed out, or dead. Most of us were motivated by fear and pain; fear of losing our families, jobs, homes, business and eventually our minds. Some come to recovery, because they are afraid they might die. Some of us came to recovery, not for fear of dying, but fearful that we wouldn't die---leaving us condemned to endure the living hell that our lives had turned into. Some come at the insistence of the court system. Some come as the results of the prayers that others had prayed, on their behalf. Some come because someone gave them this little book or some similar publication. Frequently, family members or friends watched us destroying our lives and those around us and other than praying for us they didn't have a clue of what to do to help us. So this and other publications likes this are created specifically for that purpose. It really doesn't matter how you get to recovery, what is important is that you *STAY HERE!*

If your first attempt at recovery doesn't produce what you think it should, remember that your best thinking got you in the shape that you are in! *NOW* is the time to begin to trust the thinking of others who have "been there---done that", in respect to addiction recovery. After a little success from your efforts, you will begin to trust 'some' of the people in your recovering community. You will begin to understand the wisdom of learning from those who have gone before you. As your confidence and trust in the recovery *PROCESS* grows, so will your commitment to your recovery.

Chapter Twenty

HAVING FUN

My drinking career began at age fourteen and continued until age thirty-eight. The last ten years of that included a wide variety of other drugs. Of course, I had a preference, but I would use whatever was available at the moment. Alcohol and drugs drastically affected all of my developing and impressionable years of early adulthood. Every form of enjoyment and social interaction that I knew included the use of alcohol and drugs. There were times when I drank without using drugs, but every time I used drugs I was always drinking. Needless to say, when I came into recovery at age thirty-eight, I could not imagine enjoying anything without a buzz of some kind. I could not understand how other people could enjoy life without 'partying'. Does this sound a little familiar to you?

My friend, life is not boring or dull. I haven't had to drink or drug, in quite a while. As I began to **APPLY** the tools of recovery in my life, I began to change. First, my attitude changed. Next, my thinking, habits, and eventually my whole life-style changed. Before any of the changes occurred, I first, had to become willing to try following some suggestions that seemed corny or even absurd. The longer I stayed clean and sober, the more I began to enjoy doing simple things that I had never done, as well as things that I stopped doing because I was either too broke or too stoned to enjoy them. Let's take a look at some of these activities. As you read through this list, make a check beside the ones that you have never done---but think you would like to try:

Amusement Parks
Arts and Crafts
Bicycling
Boating
Build Something
Call an Old Friend
Camping
Cooking
Creative Writing
Dancing
Dinner Theatre
Fishing
Hair Styling
Hiking
Hockey
Ice Skating
Jogging
Join a Club or Organization

Join a Gym or Health Club

Making Videos
Movies
Museums

Painting
Picnics
Plays
Playing a Musical
Instrument
Read a Book
Rock Climbing
Shopping
Skateboarding
Surfing
Swimming
Take Quiet Walks
Television
Tennis
Throwing Frisbee
Video Games
Volleyball
Volunteer at
Hospital
Volunteer at
Rest Home
Watching Videos
Working on Cars

and/or teach someone how to do one of the above or something that you do very well.

If there is something on the list that you already do well, then find someone in your recovering community, who has a similar interest, and teach them what you know. It will help both of you to stay clean and sober. *The best insurance against relapsing is working with another alcoholic or addict.* The longer you remain clean and sober, the more God will use you to help others who have not made it as far along as you have.

"We have to give it away to keep it."

Many newcomers to recovery will say, *"I have nothing to give anyone, because I'm new at this myself!"* It is true that we cannot give away something that we don't have, but let's take a look at what the newcomer does have to contribute:

The newcomer has many life experiences that were painful due to drinking/drugging. He/she my not be able to share much about their new sober living experiences, but they can share their pain and their *discoveries of what doesn't work*. When a person shares their experience, strength, and hope---or just their fear and pain---everyone in the group benefits---one way or another, whether they realize it or not. Example: A newcomer sharing their anger, fear, pain, and confusion helps the 'old timer' to remember where he/she came from. It also tells the 'old timer' that it hasn't gotten any better 'out there'. The newcomer helps others, in more ways than he/she may realize. Life's puzzle is comprised of ALL the pieces, no matter how broken some may be.

At some point in my drinking career, I lost the ability to stop, once I got started. Once I got started, I could no longer be certain of what my behavior was going to be like or in what geographical location I might 'come to' in. I became a real Jeckyl and Hyde. I traded my ability to be a husband and father for the life-style of partying and raising hell.

Whenever I am privileged to work with a newcomer. one-on-one, it is a grim reminder of where I could be if I took *'just one* or used any kind of dope *just once"*.

It is NOT the 10th or 15th drink that gets us into trouble. It is the FIRST ONE!!!

Today I am armed with the realization that once I got started, I would not have the ability to stop.

Because of the difference in our body chemistry, non-alcoholics or non-addicts do not get the same type of buzz that we get. A social drinker can stop, whenever he/she chooses and usually does before they are significantly affected. Most of us drank for the effect.

Whenever I drank I was faced with two major dilemmas: Once I started, *I COULD NOT STOP* until I was broke, locked up, passed out, or all of the above.

"I simply could not NOT DRINK, once I got started."

Toward the end of my drinking career, my behavior became totally unpredictable. I progressively became willing to go to further extremes. Although not a violent person by nature, I became very volatile and increasingly angry most of the time.

So it is a two-way deal. The newcomer helps the old-timer by keeping his memory fresh about the destructiveness of this disease and the old-timer teaches the newcomer how to get sober and *STAY SOBER*.

You must realize, that in reading this book, you are covering an awful lot of ground, in a short period of time. Much of the material, spoken here, will take you quite a while to internalize and apply. So don't try to make all of this happen quickly, because it just won't happen quickly.

Those of us who participate in a 12-step recovery program have learned to take it "one day at a time." Let's examine the wisdom of maintaining that attitude.

Staying in *TODAY* is difficult to do at times, throughout our sobriety---but especially when you are new in recovery. It may seem difficult at first, but it is very necessary. The past serves as a history lesson for us. *We learn from the past what has worked and what has not worked.* The feelings of guilt and remorse serve a purpose, at first. They are warning signals that tell us that our 'old way' just isn't working, for us, anymore. Those feelings are part of what gets our attention---long enough for us to seek relief---somewhere. Remember the 'circle of madness' that was illustrated earlier in the book. Guilt and remorse caused pain for us that was so intense we could not tolerate it. In recovery, we learn how to deal with the causes of those feelings, without having to relive the pain or numb-out. This is a process that we learn one day at a time. We can only accomplish so much in one day, so don't expect yourself to change overnight. If we walk five miles into the woods, then we have to walk five miles back out of the woods. We do not undo and redo habits and life-styles in a week or two. So be patient with yourself.

Chapter Twenty-One

GUILT AND REMORSE

1. The past cannot be undone!!!!!! So, we learn from it---with the hope that, in time, we will change sufficiently---that we will not repeat the same mistakes and make the same poor choices.

2. None of us are guaranteed that there will be a tomorrow or next week. There is nothing wrong with planning for the future, as long as we are not living for the future. Hope for a better tomorrow is a wonderful thing; however, we must recognize and remember that all we have to work with is *TODAY.*

TODAY is when I can take action. Can you take action next week? No! Can you take action yesterday? No! We can only take action *TODAY.* So, if I spend part of my day worrying about the mistakes I made yesterday and another part of this day in fear of, or trying to figure out tomorrow or next week, what have I actually accomplished? I have wasted *TODAY* worrying about things that have already happened and can't be changed, or worrying about a future that I might not have.

Let us assume that we do have a future and that better planning is necessary. We need to slow down and *PUT FIRST THINGS FIRST.* Your sobriety must come first or you won't have a future to concern yourself with.

For the active alcoholic and addict, there is only one future: *prisons, institutions, and/or death!!!!*

So today, just for today---I will not drink or use drugs *NO MATTER WHAT!!!* Whatever it takes to get through this day chemical-free, *I am willing to do whatever it takes---JUST FOR TODAY!!!!*

Then tomorrow, when it gets here, will be the next 'today' and I must say to myself, *"Today, just today, I will not drink or use drugs---no matter what I have to do to stay clean and sober.* I reserve the right to get twisted 'tomorrow', but not today. Having this attitude and applying the tools of sober living, that you are learning, is the only way---outside of a profound religious experience---that you will be able to remain chemical-free. Will power, alone, will *not* get you through the long haul.

Positive results require *POSITIVE ACTION!!!* We cannot continue doing the same old things and expect the outcome to be any different than it has been.

Before we go any further, let me share with you what happened to me at my very first AA meeting. I sat for an hour listening to people speak of things from how much of a mess their lives were in to how wonderful life had become since getting clean and sober. Truthfully, I didn't hear all of what was said at the meeting, because I was caught up in my head with all the emotional pain I was feeling at the moment. I didn't know if I belonged there or not, but I felt like I didn't belong anywhere else so I thought, *"So, why not give this a chance?"* I had lost a lot of weight. My skin was yellow. (I am Caucasian.) The whites of my eyes were turning yellow. My eyes looked like black circles recessed into my head. My clothes had become so baggy I looked like five pounds of stuff in a twenty-pound bag. I was sitting there trying to be 'cool', but I actually had a death grip on that chair---for fear of vibrating right out of it. I was, truly, in a very hopeless state of mind and body. I did not immediately feel comfortable, but I was made to feel welcome. It seemed very strange to hear them say, *"We are glad that you are here."* I had no idea why a group of strangers would be glad that I was there. In my mind, I was thinking that if they really knew how screwed up I was, they would probably be glad if I didn't come back. However, I later came to understand what they meant. It was what happened after the meeting that *literally changed my life!!!*

Immediately after the meeting, a lady walked up to me and introduced herself. She seemed kind and concerned and she welcomed me to the fellowship. She assured me that things would get better. She shared with me what a little of her life had been like, what happened, and what it was like now.

I asked her, *"How, after twenty-four years of daily drinking, do I just 'not drink' anymore?"* She asked me, *"Do you believe in God?"* I said, *"Yes."* She asked, *"Do you ever pray?"* I said, *"Yes, when my butt's on fire!"* At this point, I was willing to try anything that anyone suggested.

She said this to me: *"Go home tonight and get on your knees, beside your bed and ask God to take away from you the DESIRE AND COMPULSION TO DRINK OR DRUG. Say thank you, then shut up, and go to bed!"* That was simple enough for my frazzled mind to comprehend. She said to pray that prayer every night, for the next two weeks, and see what happens. She said that the prayer worked for her and maybe it would work for me.

Back then, I had bits and pieces of things that I had heard or read about spiritual matters. But there was very little, if anything, that I could apply. I did remember that somewhere in the scriptures it said that God wanted us to come to him like a child with a contrite heart. Well, I wasn't used to praying regularly and at the age of 38, getting on my knees by my bed did not feel natural or comfortable. But nonetheless, *I DID EXACTLY WHAT SHE SUGGESTED---EXACTLY THE WAY SHE SUGGESTED I SHOULD DO IT.* Every night thereafter, I got on my knees by my bed and asked God to take away from me the *DESIRE and COMPULSION TO DRINK or DRUG.* I then thanked Him, God, and went to bed.

One afternoon I had stopped by a little store, near my house, to buy some junk food and gas. While inside, I walked past the beer cooler and paused for a moment. As I looked at all the beer, stacked in there, and the condensation running down the glass door, I looked at my watch to check the date and *"My God, I thought to myself!!!"* I had been in this store a hundred times, during the past two weeks, and not once did I ever walk over to the cooler and romance the thought of how good a cold beer would taste. *Not once!!!* I had actually been sober for fourteen days and had not given a thought to drinking or getting high. I had been sleeping well, no shakes or jitters anymore. I was stunned with disbelief. That may not sound like much to you, but friend, that was an absolute miracle in my life!!!

The remainder of that day was spent quietly thinking and reevaluating my concept of God and the *REALITY* of the power of prayer. You see, I always believed in God, but my concept of Him was that of an all-powerful being that was too busy running the universe to be concerned with the messed up life of a skinny, worn out drunk and junkie, like me. Whenever something good happened in my life, I was quick to take the credit for it. When things went badly in my life, I was quick to blame God for letting the bad things happen.

For the first time in my life, I knew, **without a doubt,** that the simple prayer the lady taught me was the reason I had gone two weeks without ever thinking of taking a drink or drug. Keep in mind that I had become a maintenance drinker, drinking throughout the day, *EVERYDAY FOR THE PAST 24 YEARS.*

I have shared this story and her suggestion with many alcoholics and addicts since that time. Some of them have since let me know that it worked for them and some said it didn't work for them. For me, it was the beginning of a new kind of faith. Around that same time frame, someone told me that I had turned my back on God, but that He had never turned His back on me. I had felt so unworthy of God's love and on top of that, I just didn't think that God would get involved in any part of my everyday life---in a physical way. *I WAS WRONG!!!!*

The results of that little prayer was the beginning of a **NEW ATTITUDE** about a lot of things. One very important thing that I came to understand was that just because I thought, felt or believed something, did not necessarily mean that it was true. As I began to examine my thinking further, I began to discover that, most of what I thought or believed, was either distorted or incomplete. It stands to reason, when you consider that alcohol and drugs radically affected all of my developmental years. How could my thinking **NOT** have been screwed up? The longer I remained sober, the more I realized that my judgment was simply not as trustworthy as I had assumed it to be.

Keep in mind, that while going through these new levels of awareness, I was attending 12-step meetings daily. I drank and drugged daily, so I was told that I would have to put the same or more effort into my recovery process---daily, Sometimes, it was minute-by-minute. Having been fortunate enough to go through a treatment program, I learned a great deal about this "disease". I learned how cunning, baffling, powerful, and patient this enemy is. A tremendous burden was lifted from my heart, when I realized that I was not a creep trying to be a better person, but instead I was a very sick man trying desperately to get well.

The word 'alcoholism' used to stick in my throat. MY lack of knowledge of the disease allowed my ego to take control. Doing the steps, of the 12-step program, allowed the recovery process to chip away at my false pride and ego---a little at a time. I was trying to learn how to become teachable. Real recovery began, when I stopped fighting---anything and everything---and accepted the fact *this was a disease and I had it.* I came to understand that I could get addicted to anything that made me feel different than I was feeling. The daily positive reinforcement of my support system and a willingness to remain open-minded, has allowed me to recover from the "hopeless state of mind and body" that I was in before entering into recovery.

Chapter Twenty-Two

POSITIVE ACTION

Earlier we talked about **HONESTY, OPEN-MINDEDNESS, and WILLINGNESS.** I have been a musician- of-sorts for about 40 years. Do you know what I discovered? Simply: *"The more I learn, the more I realize I don't know."* I will never be able to play as well as I would like to, but I am grateful for whatever skill and talent that I have. We must learn to remain grateful for the good things in our lives, instead of dwelling on the negative.

None of us want to admit that we are powerless over anything; however, I was powerless to stop drinking and stay stopped. I was powerless to change my life for the better, because as long as I was drinking and drugging, my life was destined to go downhill.

The first step of my recovery began, when I admitted to myself, that I could **NOT** fix myself. I needed help! Humility is a necessary and admirable quality, but one which comes very slowly to alcoholics and addicts. I had been embarrassed and humiliated countless times, in my drunken life, but always bounced back---with even greater ego and false pride. However, when I wobbled into that treatment center and asked for help, I had tears in my eyes and a huge lump in my throat. There was absolutely no doubt in my mind that alcohol and drugs had beaten me to a bloody pulp and would continue to do so---unless I got help from somewhere!! The disease had literally beaten me to knees and I thank God that it did. In recovery, we call that "hitting bottom."

Some of you, like myself, will hit a low bottom and some of you will get off of the madness train, before it crashes. Some of you will die a miserable death, trying to convince yourselves that 'you can handle it'. Statistically speaking, a lot more fail than succeed at attaining long-term sobriety.

How much do you want it? How willing are you to keep trying? The apparent unmanageability of our lives should be enough to motivate us, but it usually isn't. It usually takes raw pain and sheer terror to bring us to our bottom. I pray that you have hit yours *NOW!!!!!*

After hearing and observing others in your recovering community, you will actually begin to believe that a power, greater than yourself, can restore you to sanity.

Let's review what the recovery definition of *INSANITY* is:

INSANITY IS:Repeating the same old behavior, expecting the results to be different!

We come to know that whatever our concept of God is or isn't, doesn't really matter, at first. This is because, as we remain clean and sober, that picture gets increasingly clearer.

We sometimes ask ourselves, *"Just what it is that we can believe in?"*

You can believe that: Drugs and alcohol *can and will* destroy your life and the lives of those you care about most. You are probably experiencing that now.

You can believe that: Whatever faith you can muster up now, will grow immensely---as you remain clean and sober.

104

You can believe that: If you remain open-minded, you will learn the truth of many things that you thought you knew---but were actually wrong about.

You can believe that: It is a wonderful freedom to know that your thinking was wrong and that you are not condemned to a life of pain and misery.

You can believe that: Until your faith grows, your daily participation in a support group of recovering people will help you get through the rough spots.

You can believe that: There is no room in your recovery for indifference and prejudice. Participate in your recovery with open-minded optimism, not judgmental pessimism.

You can believe that: Trying to intellectualize your way through recovery will get you drunk. *"KEEP IT SIMPLE!""*

You can believe that: If you forget what you think you know about living life and remain open-minded, you will learn how to live a life a completely different way *AND* enjoy it more than ever before.

You can believe that: Feelings of self-sufficiency will get you drunk. What I mean by that is, if we possessed the ability to heal ourselves of this disease, we all would have done that---long before hitting our bottom. *It is a power greater than us that brings about the healing. Our job is to learn how to endure the process.*

You can believe that: If in prayer, you ask for the strength to endure the processes, you will be given the strength and the perseverance you need.

You can believe that: Negative people and negative thinking will always yield negative results: just as positive people and positive thinking will always yield positive results.

You can believe that: Defiance is an outstanding and somewhat normal characteristic of alcoholics and addicts. We do not normally gravitate toward change of any kind, without some degree of resistance and/or procrastination. The resistance and procrastination are fairly strong at first; however, as our faith in the recovery process grows, these barriers diminish. At first, we resist following suggestions to the letter--- defiance. We seem to take them in small increments, until we begin to see the results in others in our support group. We will usually not see change in ourselves, as quickly as others see in us.

You can believe that: If you apply everything you have learned in this publication, you will get very excited about sobriety.

If you can believe the things that I have just presented to you, then you can believe that you are at a rallying point to sanity and that you are on the road to a new and wonderful life, as well as a new relationship with God.

PRAYER:

When I was in active addiction, my prayers went something like this:

"Well God, I'm in a mess again, but here is how we need to straighten it out: I need to do this and this. You need to do this and this---and here is what I think would be best. So, I want YOU to help me pull it off."

Does this sound a little familiar? Well, here is what my, not necessarily yours, prayers may sound like today:

"Precious Father in Heaven, forgive me I pray, for I have been sinful in thought, word, and deed. I repent of my sins and transgressions against thee and ask for your forgiveness. Father, I thank you for your love and mercy. Show me how to live this day as you would have me live it and grant me, I pray, the willingness, courage, ability, and desire to live this day as you direct me, that all success would bring glory to thy name. In Jesus' name, I praise and thank you Father. Amen."

Now before you start doing cheetah-flips and monkey-rolls about that prayer, remember I said that this was *MY* prayer. By all means, pray however you wish! But if your prayers haven't been getting you anywhere, then try mine. *IT WORKS FOR ME!!!!*

You most definitely do not have to be Christian to recover, anymore so than you have to be a Christian to suffer from alcoholism/addiction. Whatever your faith and beliefs or lack of faith or beliefs, if you *APPLY* what you have learned in this text, you *CAN SUCCEED* in your recovery!!!!!!!!!!!!!!!!!!!!!!!!

On my desk is a King James Bible, NIV-Study Bible, the Koran, the I-ching, the Tao-Te-Ching, and the Bhagvad-Gita. My personal library contains a number of other types of esoteric and metaphysical literature. There is great value in all Holy Scriptures.

Recovery doesn't require us to believe in anything. It only requires that we have a sincere desire to stop drinking and using drugs. I have examined many religions and philosophies, some at great length. It took many years, but I eventually returned to the faith of my youth with a greater hunger for God's closeness. *YOUR JOURNEY IS YOUR OWN!!!!!!!!*

SERVICE:

Another part of *POSITIVE ACITON* is being of service to others. At first, there isn't a whole lot we can do for others, because we are struggling to adjust--- ourselves.

There are some things that we can do, when we are new. We can show up for the meetings early to help set up for the meeting. Ashtrays need to be cleaned. Tables and chairs need to be cleaned or dusted. The coffee needs to be made. Bathrooms should be clean and neat. The appropriate literature should be gotten out and arranged. Sometimes, it is nice to have a greeter at the door. Being a greeter not only makes people feel welcomed, but also gives the greeter the opportunity to get to know the other members of the group. If you have a vehicle, you might offer a ride to someone who doesn't have one. It is also important to make a list of names and phone numbers of group members and *MAKE* yourself call someone occasionally, daily when you are new. This is hard to do at first, but it gets easier, especially when we begin to realize that the person we call, whether newcomer or old-timer, is glad to hear from us and it lifts their spirit as well as our own.

With daily practice, these new disciplines become healthy habits. All of the disciplines talked about in this book will eventually define who we are. We will either become the product of continued confusion or we become spiritually fit and strong as the result of the new disciplines we have been taught, over time while young in our recovery. We find that we have ventured into a wonderful process of learning and growing physically and spiritually fit. We have become a student of life, studying a course in metaphysics that we will never graduate from. We simply continue growing, changing, and helping others to get another chance at changing their lives.

The daily maintenance of our spiritual condition is absolutely essential, in order for us to remain clean and sober. Through prayer and participation in our local recovering community, we learn how to develop and maintain this spiritual condition. It is this spiritual condition, which allows us to accept the things we cannot change and gives us the courage to change the things we can. We learn to dwell in the positive, instead of getting caught up in the negative. Difficulties, effort, and pain are just required elements our growth process.

THE FAMILY:

This disease allows no one to escape unharmed. It affects every family member, in some way. The alcoholic/addict and his/her family find that stopping the use of alcohol and/or drugs is only the beginning of a change that will take time for all concerned to benefit from. Resentments and anger from the past, need to be put behind you, as much as possible, and replaced with and attitude of love, tolerance, and a willingness to try to be understanding toward each other. This is easier said than done **AND** it will take time. So, give time 'time'. Don't try to rush the process. For the first few months, things may not be smooth sailing, but hang in there, *because it will change*.

The alcoholic/addict knows quite well that he/she is to blame for a lot of devastation. It may take many years to repair the damage done, both financially and emotionally. The family focus should be more on the progress being made by the recovering person rather than the financial repair.

It is natural for us to want to forget the miseries of the past, because of the intense emotional pain that we are suffering during early recovery. It is no picnic, but we all had to go through it. We need to be forgiving of the past, but we don't need to forget it. We learn valuable lessons from the pain of our mistakes. For us, pain is one of our chief motivators.

As family members heal, they will encounter other people in their community who are facing the same struggles, but may not be as far along in their readjustment. Alanon is a 12-step support group for families and loved ones who need help, as much as the addict/alcoholic. The more experienced family members are given the opportunity to help new struggling families in recovery by sharing their experience, strength, and hope.

By sharing our past with others, we make it possible for them to understand and cope with the difficulties and tragedies that we had to learn 'the hard way'. Above all, family members who have been in their recovery process for a while can offer the new family **HOPE** by sharing with them how their lives have changed and improved since they began their journey.

In many cases, our painful past becomes our greatest asset throughout our recovery. This is especially true, when we begin to work with newcomers. Some transgressions may be hard to forgive, when dealing with the difficulties of trying to repair relationships. In some cases, this requires husbands and wives to separate for a while, in order for some healing and forgiveness to occur. Everyone has the right to be wrong. Just as everyone has the right to feel and process their own pain and anger. Most of the time family members need *TIME* and *SPACE* to simply process their feelings. They are damaged too. They also have a lot of adjusting and readjusting to do. *"Easy does it!"* Do not try to rush the healing process, especially that of others.

ONCE ISSUES HAVE BEEN DISCUSSED AND RESOLVED, THEY SHOULD NOT BE BROUGHT BACK UP IN ANGER AT A LATER TIME!!

A recovering person may criticize or laugh at himself or herself and it may have a favorable effect on himself and/or others; however, such criticism coming from others may cause great harm. People who are in early recovery are very thin-skinned and have a tendency to personalize everything they hear. Family members should try to be a little cautious and considerate of the fact that people in early recovery are easily frightened or offended. This emotional state is a normal part of their physical healing. As the brain's neuro-chemistry returns to its normal state of functioning, the recovering person gradually becomes much less emotionally fragile.

The longer the person remains clean and sober, the more stable their emotions become. The emotional roller coaster will pass. *REMEMBER, this is a process and IT TAKES TIME!! So, BE PATIENT!!!!!!!!!*

Addicts and alcoholics are obsessive-compulsive, by nature, and do everything to extremes. It is normal for the newly recovering person to go overboard, at first. Sometimes, they put so much emphasis on their recovery and financial repair that they neglect their family. With understanding and encouragement, through positive communication and support, the recovering person will eventually find a compatible balance. When patience run short, the recovering person's family should remember what the alcoholic/addict was like before entering recovery. Again, we need to focus on the progress being made, not the difficulties, which **always** precede progress. The best way to bring about some balance is for the family to talk **calmly and peacefully.** If family talks can be carried on **without** blaming, arguments, self-pity, anger, or criticism, then real progress can be made. All of the pain, fear, anger, and confusion are still fresh in the family members minds; therefore, it may take a while for these talks to come together calmly and peacefully. Frequently, the family members of the recovering person realize that their expectations of change for their recovering family member is and has been unrealistic for where the recovering person is in their very early recovery. With most of us, change comes slowly and with great effort. It takes time!

The recovering person, on the other hand, may experience a moving or profound spiritual experience, which may take him/her on a temporary journey of religious fanaticism or energetic pursuit. It is common for the newcomer to experience a very heightened state of awareness and well-being. Likewise, it is common for the person experiencing this to go over-board trying to share with or give to his family members and friends---this new profound direction his/her life is taking. Sometimes the recovering person's constant enthusiasm causes them to become a pest to their family and friends. Try to keep in mind that this period of super-enthusiasm is a phase and will eventually level out. However, the values and spiritual principles, by which the recovering person is patterning his/her life, have been long tested and proven to be well worthy of family examination. Just remember, that as long as the newcomer is in this phase of transition, he /she is most likely to remain clean and sober.

As with other stages of development, the newcomer may spend what seems to be an unreasonable amount of time exploring this new **SPIRITUAL AWARENESS** to the point of again neglecting the needs of the family. A good sponsor will recognize this and step in to help the newcomer get back to a state of balance. Eventually, the newcomer realizes that the family obligations and everyday responsibilities are a part of the **SPIRITUAL DIRECTION** that the recovering person is gravitating toward. In many instances, families are brought together with shared values and the implementation of new and more profound spiritual values, which serve them well in rebuilding their new lives together.

As the recovering person begins to venture 'back into the world' again, he/she may begin to show interests in doing more normal things for recreation. Even if the family is not particularly interested, they should make an effort to participate in some type of recreation with the recovering family member. Eventually, finding and participating in a local religious fellowship is often helpful to all concerned.

Low energy level and periodic cravings are not uncommon for the newly recovering person. It has been suggested that we keep a supply of chocolate on hand, since the chocolate will ease the cravings, as well as give the person a little boost of energy.

SEXUAL DIFFICULTIES:

It is very common for males, in addiction and in early recovery, to experience impotence or diminished sexual desire. Do not be alarmed, if you should experience this during your early recovery. You must keep in mind that your body chemistry and emotional state are going through some very profound changes. This difficulty usually corrects itself within a few months--- after which we commonly enjoy a much greater degree of intimacy and much improved sexual endurance and performance. If impotence remains a problem after several months of recovery, it might be a good idea to consult a physician.

CHILDRENS' RELUCTANCE TO FORGIVE:

It is not uncommon for children to either **STUFF** their feelings or act-out---displaying behavior which could lead to serious problems later. They, too, have been hurt, neglected, and frightened by the consequences of this disease. They need time and help in dealing with their feelings. Given some time and help, we frequently find that family members display a measure of forgiveness that amazes us. Some are quick to forgive and for some, it takes a while for a little healing to occur. The alcoholic/addict has had a well-established track record of screwing up and causing pain; therefore, it takes some time and **CONSISTENT** quality recovery to regain the trust of family members and friends.

When I was 'out there' drinking and using drugs, my family never knew whether I would come home and pass out---or whether I would come home acting like a raving lunatic. They were accustomed to absolute inconsistency and unpredictability. So naturally, to protect their own emotions, they became withdrawn and reluctant to be around me. Sobriety gave back to me some consistency, my dignity, and the love and respect of my family members---but it took *TIME* and a lot of *HARD WORK*. I have found that with most of us, family members want to forgive us, but they are afraid of letting down their emotional guard for fear that we will return to the old life-style, as we always have in the past---after failed attempts at straightening out our lives. *TIME* is a major factor in the healing *PROCESS* so be as patient with each other as you possibly can.

The family members frequently choose to join their recovering counter-part in a more focused spiritual way of living. If so, the family unity will certainly begin to reflect such a wise decision. On the other hand, not all families choose to join their recovering counter-part in their spiritual journey. "Different strokes for different folks." The recovering person *MUST,* at any cost, continue living their life on a spiritual basis---if they are to remain free from alcohol and drugs. It is necessary for all to adopt the attitude of *"live and let live."* Mutual respect and tolerance are necessary for everyone, when it comes to their spiritual beliefs or disbeliefs. Everyone chooses their own direction and spiritually matures at their own pace.

If the recovering person remains sober and spiritually focused, their children not only forgive them, but also frequently join their recovering parent in their daily disciplines, which can contribute to the continued expansion of their spiritual horizons.

IN CLOSING:

It is **IMPOSSIBLE** for me to convey every thought and feeling that I have about **RECOVERY.** It is my sincere prayer that somewhere in these pages you read something that helps you understand the complexity of this disease and the difficulties faced by all who are affected. My prayer is that you will **CONTINUE TAKING POSITIVE ACITON,** either for yourself or for those whom you care about that are still suffering.

Chapter Twenty-Three

EDUCATION – APPLICATION - ADAPTATION

So learn as much as you can about this disease and about recovery. Then, use your support elements to help you learn how to *APPLY* what you learn, whether you like it or not!!

I *STRONGLY* encourage the suffering alcoholic/addict to seek medical assistance in the early days of detoxification. If there is adequate health insurance or financial means, I suggest that the alcoholic/addict participate in some form of in-patient treatment. This may last from three to six weeks, depending on the individual's circumstances. If in-patient treatment is not possible, then look into an outpatient program followed up with what is called 'after care'. This usually encompasses anywhere from four to twelve meetings a month, with the recovering person's primary counselor and/or group. Outpatient treatment usually last about three months, with the after-care program also lasting about three months. Depending on the local treatment facility's capabilities, these outpatient treatment programs, as well as the after-care programs, are very effective and have a good rate of success in assisting the newcomer in developing a firm foundation. It is recommended that while a person attends an outpatient treatment program, he/she should also attend AA/NA meetings during the same time frame.

Treatment is for EDUCATION.

Your twelve-step support group is for APPLICATION.

It all goes together---hand in hand.

Chapter Twenty-Four

COMMUNITY RESOURCES

1. Your local outreach phone number, which is usually in your local phone directory.

2. Your local Alcoholics Anonymous, Narcotics Anonymous, Alanon, and other 12-step groups can be found in most phone directories.

3. Your local hospital emergency room.

4. Your local Mental Health Services will be of great service. Many local Mental Health Services have a separate department especially for Family Recovery. Your local Mental Health office should also have a list of various services and facilities that are located in your immediate area.

5. Your local Police Department. Times are changing and so are the general attitudes of the public about addictive disorders. The police are much more supportive of helping the addict/alcoholic. They would much rather help us find help than just lock us up. The are usually knowledgeable of local resources in their community and are all happy to point us in a helpful direction.

If all of this material presented here seems a bit overwhelming, **DO NOT BE DISCOURAGED!** You have the rest of your life to practice what you are learning.

No one begins recovery with an ability to digest and apply everything in this book. So, don't expect yourself or anyone else to be able to. Take it easy---One Day At

A Time. Reread and apply what you can, as you are able to. Just get busy doing something. *DO NOT TRY TO ORCHESTRATE YOUR OWN RECOVERY*!!!!!!!!

WE DON'T GUARANTEE THAT FOLLOWING THE SUGGESTIONS IN THIS BOOK WILL OPEN THE DOORS OF HEAVEN AND LET YOU IN, BUT THEY WILL OPEN THE DOORS OF HELL AND LET YOU OUT!!!!!!!!!

May God continue to bless you and strengthen you and your family throughout your *NEW LIFE!!!*

Best wishes for a brighter life,

Craig L. Bradley

About the Author

The author's foremost qualification is that he is recovered from 24 years of alcoholism and addiction. He has been employed as a counselor at private treatment centers in North Carolina.

He has served as the executive director of a corporation, which owns and operates a number of halfway houses. He authored and instructed an out patient treatment program for "high risk" clients of the Federal Department of Probation.

He was instrumental in the formation of "Recovery Through Christ"; a Christian based twelve-step recovery program for alcoholics and addicts. Our author has been utilized by the local court system as an "expert witness" in cases involving felony substance abuse cases.

He assists local churches and pastors in establishing Christian outreach programs. He continues to assist local mental health programs with support for "high risk" and felony juvenile's offenders. He has spent the last seventeen years trying to give back what was given to him.

www.ingramcontent.com/pod-product-compliance
Lightning Source LLC
Chambersburg PA
CBHW051427280526
45785CB00003B/1193